Heart of Courage

Daughters of the King
Bible Study Series

Endorsements

People are talking about Kathy Collard Miller's Daughters of the King Bible Study Series and Choices of the Heart.

Kathy Collard Miller's *Choices of the Heart* is a Bible study full of sound scriptural principles, balanced spiritual wisdom, and a deep understanding of what matters most to women. Miller's study makes great use of an all-star, all female cast of leaders falling on both sides of the spiritual and moral equation. Her insightful questions invite the reader to reflect on her own life within a scriptural framework—prompting growth from the heart. I can't wait to use *Choices of the Heart* with my own women's Bible study. I'm looking forward to more from Kathy Collard Miller!
—**Catherine Finger, Ed.D,** speaker and author of the *Murder with a Message* series

With each lesson, I was invited to recognize that choices of the heart aren't simple or defined without the grace of God. Each account of women in the Bible in this Bible study lifts a layer of possible misconception, asserts refreshing challenges, and presents applications of God's Word, bold yet gentle. At times, the reader is tugged to examine the heart and analyze motives. But with each lesson, the exhortation is profoundly clear, leaving a pleasant reassurance that we women today do have much in common with women of the Bible. Yet, we are called to learn from their examples to make godly choices as daughters of the King who dance to the melody of his redeeming love.
—**Janet Perez Eckles,** author of *Simply Salsa: Dancing Without Fear at God's Fiesta*

Choices of the Heart from bestselling author Kathy Collard Miller is a must-read for all women who desire to

walk in God's light as they become more like Jesus. This is not only a well-written book, but it is also laid out in such a way that it can be used by both individuals and groups. Highly recommended!
—**Kathi Macias,** multi-award-winning author of more than fifty books, including *The Singing Quilt* and *Return to Christmas* www.kathimacias.com

Kathy Collard Miller's new study, *Choices of the Heart*, gives us a treasure chest of encouragement and wisdom for a glorious life. Whether we struggle with the grittiness of jealousy, temptation or unforgiveness, Kathy points us to God who always gives us the power to move us into a meaningful pathway. I love the way Kathy takes the participant through the journey of examining the lives of women in the Bible and revealing the outcome of their bad and wise choices.

This is a great study for personal reflection during a devotion time or for discussions in a larger group setting. Kathy has done stellar research and written a masterpiece crafted to enrich the reader's knowledge of the Bible and their spiritual life.
—**Heidi McLaughlin,** international speaker and author of *Sand to Pearls*, *Beauty Unleashed* and *Restless for More*, www.heartconnection.ca

At the crux of every circumstance, we have two basic choices: whether to trust and whether to obey—intentional decisions to yield to God and embrace his Word. Kathy captures this powerful truth in *Choices of the Heart*. She invites us to walk with God in the great adventure of life, encouraged along the journey by our Heavenly Father's love and faithfulness. Such a motivating study!
—**Dawn Wilson,** founder of Heart Choices Today, San Diego, California, President of Network of Evangelical Women in Ministry (NEWIM)

Kathy Collard Miller thoughtfully addresses choices and attitudes that undermine or set us free. With encouragement and warmth, she helps us choose God's way and blessing. This exploration of biblical lives and choices can change your life.

—Judith Couchman, author of *Designing a Woman's Life* book, Bible study, and seminar

As the founder of Modern Day Princess Ministries, I am always looking to recommend resources for women that further the depth of our walk with Christ. The Daughter of the King series by Kathy Collard Miller does exactly that. It enables you to discover the wealth you have in knowing the King of Kings as your Heavenly Father and begin walking in the royalty you possess.

Doreen Hanna, Treasured Celebrations, founder www.moderndayprincess.net

Choices of the Heart provides excellent insight and instruction for the Christian woman who longs for more of God's Word. The women of the Bible come alive as they tackle life issues and struggles that are relevant to today's world. Kathy Collard Miller is a name you can trust for great Bible teaching.

—Laura Petherbridge, speaker and author of *The Smart Stepmom*, *101 Tips for The Smart Stepmom*, and *When I Do Becomes I Don't—Practical Steps for Healing During Separation and Divorce*

Heart of Courage

Daughters of the King
Bible Study Series

KATHY COLLARD MILLER

Copyright Notice

Heart of Courage: Daughters of the King Bible Study Series

First edition. Copyright © 2022 by Kathy Collard Miller. The information contained in this book is the intellectual property of Kathy Collard Miller and is governed by United States and International copyright laws. All rights reserved. No part of this publication, either text or image, may be used for any purpose other than personal use. Therefore, reproduction, modification, storage in a retrieval system, or retransmission, in any form or by any means, electronic, mechanical, or otherwise, for reasons other than personal use, except for brief quotations for reviews or articles and promotions, is strictly prohibited without prior written permission by the publisher.

Scripture quotations are from the ESV. Bible (The Holy Bible, English Standard Version.), copyright 2001 by Crossway, a publishing ministry of Good News Publishers. Used by permission. All rights reserved.

Cover and Interior Design: Derinda Babcock

Editor(s): Susan K. Stewart, Deb Haggerty

PUBLISHED BY: Elk Lake Publishing, Inc., 35 Dogwood Drive, Plymouth, MA 02360, 2022

Library Cataloging Data

Names: Miller, Kathy Collard (Kathy Collard Miller)

Heart of Courage: Daughters of the King Bible Study Series / Kathy Collard Miller

196 p. 23cm × 15cm (9in × 6 in.)

Identifiers: ISBN-13: 978-1-64949-513-6 (paperback) | 978-1-64949-514-3 (trade paperback)

| 978-1-64949-515-0 (e-book)

Key Words: courage, Bible study, women, obeying God, life skills, seeking God, knowing God

Library of Congress Control Number: 2022934056

Jennifer Phillips

My forever friend, you have inspired me from the first time I met you so many years ago. Thank you for your example of courageously living life to the hilt because you trust God in spite of many challenges. I love you.

Contents

Dedication vii
Acknowledgments ix
Introduction xi

—Lesson 1—
Courage Representing God 1

—Lesson 2—
Courageous in Serving 15

—Lesson 3—
Courageously Overcoming Discouragement 33

—Lesson 4—
Courageous Within My Family 49

—Lesson 5—
Courageous in My Church 65

—Lesson 6—
Courageously Standing Against Popular Opinion . . . 85

—Lesson 7—
Courageously Standing Against Evil 101

—Lesson 8—
Courageously Standing
for God at Work 119

—Lesson 9—
Courageously Facing Temptation 139

—Lesson 10—
Courageous Jesus,
Our Inspiration 159

About the Author 179
Endnotes 181
Books by Kathy Collard Miller with Elk Lake
Publishing, Inc. 183

Acknowledgments

Back in the 1990s, Mary Nelson of Accent Publications saw the potential of my idea for a women's Bible study series. With her guidance, the twelve-book study in the "Daughters of the King Bible Study Series" was created. I was grateful for her leadership.

Now I'm thrilled Deb Haggerty has understood and supported my vision of expanding the initial simple format to include commentary and greater depth for every book in the series. Thank you, Deb. Your leadership of Elk Lake Publishing is phenomenal, and you are the Publisher of the Year in my book! You bless me with confidence and encouragement.

Susan K. Stewart is always a delight to work with as she edits and wisely guides me toward clearly communicating the truths of Scripture. Susan, you have a gentle yet skillful ability, and I so appreciate your responsiveness.

I'm so grateful for the love and encouragement from my husband, Larry. Honey, let's make it another fifty years walking this journey together. You make God look good.

Introduction

I'm so thrilled you have chosen this Bible study. I trust the Holy Spirit will enlighten you about God's courage within you, inspire you to know God wants you to live with courage, and empower you to choose courageous actions because of your increased trust in him.

I primarily used the English Standard Version (ESV) as the basis for asking questions. You may use any version you prefer, of course, but sometimes, if the wording of a particular version doesn't answer a question, you might find it beneficial to refer to the ESV.

~Lesson 1~
Courage Representing God

Influencing our world means representing God in everything we do. We don't have to be in full-time Christian service or in any leadership position to do that. We can courageously represent God in the simplest or most complex activity of each day.

Every one of those activities involves choices requiring courage to some degree. We might need God's courage to discipline our child with patience. Or bring up a touchy topic with our husband. Or tell the difficult truth in the workplace. We fight fear and wonder about the consequences of following God, especially when the people hearing us are those who have no interest in God or his kingdom kind of living. Even those claiming to be Christians can react defensively.

The fabulous news is God wants to empower us with his courage. He will not leave us without his resources. He is the wisdom needed to fulfill his plan for our every choice no matter how difficult.

In this first lesson, let's look at an overall view of being courageous for God and empowered by him for representing him. And then, in our other lessons, we will explore specific topics in more detail. In this study, we will look both at what courage is and how to view it with a godly perspective.

Can we have confidence living with courage is possible—and God's will? Absolutely. By seeking him more and more through studying his Word, we will grow stronger in obeying and drawing closer to our loving God.

1. How do you define courage?

2. Do you think it takes courage to serve God? Why or why not?

3. What does it mean to you to represent God?

    A. In what ways have you represented God?

    At home:

    At work:

    At church:

    In the community:

B. If you don't think you represent God, why do you believe that?

Courage can be defined as the ability and persevering strength to act regardless of the obvious or perceived danger. As Christians, we would include taking the godly, correct action that represents God in truth.

Every person has a different level of ability to act courageously when faced with challenges and difficulties based upon temperament/personality, culture, childhood experiences, belief system, training, and physical health. Yet when God tells us in the Bible to take ahold of his courage like in Joshua 1:9, he never mentions any limitations or influences. His courage is strong enough to overcome anything hindering us. He tells us nothing is impossible with him (Luke 1:37).

4. Read 2 Corinthians 5:9–21.

A. What are at least five motivating factors for representing God (vs. 9–14a)?

-
-
-
-
-

B. How do you think living courageously for God relates to no longer living for ourselves (2 Corinthians 5:14–15)?

C. How do you think being a new person in Christ relates to no longer living for ourselves (vs. 17)?

As with all Bible passages, there is always context and background history occurring "behind the scenes." Almost every epistle (a New Testament "letter" to a group of believers or an individual) is intended to address some issue. In his first letter to the Corinthians, Paul addresses the problems the Corinthian believers are experiencing, one of which is not standing up courageously against false teachers. These false teachers have begun to influence the believers with lies about Paul's methods and his message of salvation through Jesus's death and resurrection (I Corinthians 15:3–4).

In this section, 2 Corinthians 5:9–2, Paul is trying to point out how he himself has the courage to stand up for God in the face of misunderstanding and opposition. The same reasons he gives are ones that can encourage us to stand strong for God.

These reasons are desire to please God (v. 9), God's judgment (v. 10), fearing God (v. 11), having a conscience (v. 11), knowing how to stand against false teachers (v. 12), willingness to be called crazy (v. 13), and being empowered by God's love for others (v. 14).

Paul risked everything in his ministry in many ways—often even facing endless difficulties and leadership challenges. Empowered by God's courage, he was willing to serve at the cost of his own comfort. What a wonderful reminder of Jesus, who experienced the same things and gave his innocent blood for our salvation (vs. 14–15).

Often, we begin to be discouraged realizing our needs aren't being met. Then we must remember Jesus, who sacrificed his own needs. Instead, his only desire was to selflessly and courageously please his Heavenly Father and fulfill his purpose of saving his chosen people. Such sacrificial obedience cost him leaving the joys of heaven, suffering as a human with human emotions and trials—being misunderstood, wrongly accused, and rejected by his disciples. And then, finally, dying on the behalf of sinners even though he had never sinned.

> 5. In the dictionary, look up "reconciliation" and "reconcile." Write the definitions here.
>
> A. How do those definitions relate to what Paul is talking about in 2 Corinthians 5:18–21?
>
> B. Based on the definition of the word "reconciliation" and the information given in verses 18–21, how would you explain the concept to an unbeliever who wants to know God yet feels she must earn reconciliation with God?

One beautiful definition of reconciliation is restoring harmony. The need for reconciliation between God and humanity began in the Garden of Eden when Adam and Eve disobeyed God. Before they disobeyed, they were naked and experienced no shame. When they sinned, they knew they were guilty. Then they tried to cover their shame with fig leaves.

Of course, God knew everything occurring in his garden and reached out to this hurting couple—covered with ineffective leaves. They hid—he pursued them. He pursued *them!*

Because God always knew his created beings would sin, he planned the reconciliation. He killed an animal and clothed this man and woman with something more permanent. The animal's spilled blood represented the coming Messiah who would shed his blood as the totally effective and permanent means of reconciliation.

Jesus's sacrifice is the means of reconciliation Paul wants the Corinthians to remember. If they do, they can fight the lies from the false teachers who had devised their own self-righteous ways of gaining acceptance from God.

6. How did the following women represent God courageously?

Verses	**Woman**	**How she represented God**
Exodus 15:20–21; Micah 6:4		
Judges 4:4–6		
Judges 4:17–22		
2 Kings 22:14–20		
Esther 4:12–16		

Verses	Woman	How she represented God
John 4:28–30		
Acts 16:14–15		

    A. Do you relate to any of those women? In what way?

    B. What is the most important encouragement or instruction you gain from these women?

7. What foundations for courageous service for God are named in Colossians 3:17, 23–24?

We might tend to believe only certain responsibilities are valuable for serving God. We sometimes think being "in the ministry" is only what's valuable. We conclude "just" being a mom, or having a job, or being available for the needs of grandchildren can't count as God's service. We also might value certain "spiritual gifts" as more important than others. We can think gifts like hospitality can't offer much value. But everything God gives as opportunities to represent him are significant in his plan and require focusing on glorifying God and diminishing making it about "me."

8. What wrong attitudes do these verses warn us about?

   A. Numbers 12:1–2:

   B. Proverbs 24:1–2, 19–20:

   C. Mark 12:38–40:

   D. Galatians 6:3:

   E. Ephesians 4:31:

   F. Philippians 2:3:

   G. 2 Timothy 2:16:

God is interested in the motives of our hearts. What energizes our service is as important as whether we are obeying. We should evaluate our hearts and be teachable. We should be willing to allow the Holy Spirit to reveal any jealousy, pride, envy, insecurity, and self-protection. When we ask for his forgiveness, he forgives and cleanses us (1 John 1:9). Out of our renewed pure heart, we can rightly discern how he wants us to courageously proceed.

9. How do these verses indicate God wants to strengthen our courage to serve him from a purer heart? What does each passage mean to you in practical terms?

The first one is completed for you.

Verse(s)	Instruction	Practical meaning
I Corinthians 3:10	Build as God gives grace.	Don't be jealous if someone else is building on what I began.
I Corinthians 9:22–23		
I Corinthians 9:25		
Ephesians 6:10–11		
I Timothy 4:12		
I Timothy 4:14–15		
II Timothy 2:15		
II Timothy 2:22–26		
II Timothy 3:16–17		

First Timothy 4:15 offers a unique perspective of the journey of learning courage. Verse 15 tells us, "Practice these things, immerse yourself in them, so that all may see your progress." The Greek word for progress, *prokopē*, is the idea of "cut forward" or "advance." God is encouraging us to continue growing a little at a time. Often, we become discouraged (a lack of courage), because we experience failure or not having the results we think God expects from us. We haven't arrived, and we think God is impatient.

Some of us believe God wants us to attain perfection on earth. But God didn't cause Timothy to write, "so that all may see your *perfection*." God inspired him to write, "so that all may see your *progress*." Knowing God's realistic expectations strengthens our courage to persevere and trust God for little-by-little growth.

10. Since we can't perfectly live in God's provision of courage, how do these verses encourage you to continue serving God?

    A. Philippians 1:6:

    B. Hebrews 4:15:

    C. Hebrews 10:14:

    D. I John 1:8, 10:

    E. I John 1:9:

11. From the following verses in Romans, what attitudes and instructions help you influence your world more effectively as you courageously represent God?

   A. 1:16:

   B. 8:26–27, 31:

   C. 12:1–2:

   D. 12:9–10:

   E. 12:14–15:

   F. 12:16:

   G. 12:17–21:

   H. 14:10–13, 19:

   I. 15:1:

   J. 15:5–7:

12. How will these attitudes make you more courageous?

13. Which one is most important to you for your current challenge?

Let's focus on Romans 14 as an example of influencing others. All of Romans 14 is a guidebook for loving in wise ways as we courageously represent God. The apostle Paul is helping Jesus followers correct their wrong practices of passing judgment on those who believe differently about what kinds of food are allowed for believers. They aren't being kind, patient, and loving.

God is not glorified by their impatience. They may think they are being courageous, but they aren't representing God accurately. They are putting a "stumbling block" and "hindrance" (v. 13) in the way of some Christians. The Greek word for a stumbling block, *proskomma*, is the visual of something in the road. If a person's foot hits it, she could stumble or fall. This visual describes what can happen in a person's heart when she is feeling peace about something, but then she hears someone's criticism, and her courage dissipates. She condemns herself and might even doubt her salvation or her commitment to Christ. Her faith falters, and she spends time worrying about her walk with Christ over something insignificant.

Silence is sometimes the wiser course (verse 22). If we truly are courageous, we will have enough trust in God to know God can create change in someone's beliefs—even without our input. If we have confidence in God's power, we will be able to hear more clearly how God wants us to interact with that person.

    14. Is there any way God wants you to be courageous for him, yet you've hesitated?

        A. What attitude(s) do you need to obey God?

        B. What will you do to demonstrate your courage for God in that area this week?

We have begun the journey of being more aware of the motives at the root of a courageous heart. The foundation is based on wanting "an audience" of one, our Lord God Almighty.

We are not without help in this journey. God wants to strengthen our selflessness through the instruction and empowering of his indwelling Holy Spirit. The foundation begins by being assured we are reconciled with God because of the sacrificial death of Jesus, his Son, our Messiah.

Then we can courageously serve our God with joy and confidence knowing our reward is waiting for us in heaven, even if we aren't applauded here on earth.

My Precious Princess and Daughter:

I see and know the courage laying within your heart, which I put there. It delights me to use you and your special gifts in unique ways I have planned uniquely for you. Don't compare yourself to others. My plan for you gives you freedom in the way you will tell others about me. My greatness is not destroyed by any inadequacies of my children. I have given you abilities and talents, which I will use in the best possible way.

You represent me. I am pleased with you my daughter, my princess. I know you sometimes fail. But I also know the desire of your heart to show others my love for them. Do not doubt my desire to have you represent me.

I am working in your life as you grow ever wiser in being my ambassador. I give all my children courageous hearts. But some refuse to accept my courage as the foundation for all they do. Let me supply the courage you need to stand for me.

Lovingly,
Your Heavenly Father, the King

~Lesson 2~
Courageous in Serving

God gave women an inborn desire to help others, and to nurture and invest from the heart. Yes, of course, men want to do the same, but most often, a man influences others in a different way. They prefer "fixing" and solving.

There's no one way to help or serve. God has created us uniquely with different strengths and weaknesses regardless of our gender. What a great plan since there are a variety of needs around us.

Only God is sufficient for every need, but he chooses to use us to partner with him in meeting particular needs. He never intended for one person, you or I, to meet every need for every person. He wants us to operate within the body of Christ with different giftings.

With this in mind, let's look at God's viewpoint of courageously serving as the Bible declares.

1. In what ways have other Christians ministered to you?

2. What struggles or difficulties have you faced in trying to help others?

3. Read 1 Kings 17:8–24.

   A. Do you think this widow personally knew the God Elijah represented (v. 12)?

   B. Why do you think she had a commitment to do what Elijah said?

   C. How was her service to Elijah sacrificial and revealed her attitude about serving (vs. 13)?

   D. What wrong assumptions did this widow have about Elijah and his motives (v. 18)?

   E. How did God bless this widow (vv. 22–24)?

At the time God commands Elijah to go to Zarephath, the drought had been going on for six months. The drought was God's judgment upon the people of Israel to motivate them to turn from various sins including worshipping and trusting in other gods, like Baal. One of the primary reasons the people had turned away from Jehovah was because of the evil influence from Queen Jezebel, who is married to King Ahab. She is from the nearby pagan country of Sidon. She created locations, called "high places," for the Israelites to worship her primary god, Baal, who was believed to be the storm god. The people of Sidon believed when there wasn't rain, Baal had died and would come back to life later—if they did certain things.

God chose a lack of rain for their judgment specifically to make the point he controlled the weather, not the false god Baal. Everything God does has a purpose to teach about who he is and how we should respond to him. Ironically, the drought spread to the very country where Baal, the storm god, was worshipped. God was multi-tasking.

Even though God was penalizing his people to draw them back to himself, he took care of his prophet, Elijah. In a most unlikely move, God sent him to Israel's enemy territory, the country of Phoenician Sidon, where the wicked Jezebel grew up. Elijah must have been challenged to believe God would take care of him among his enemies.

God's secondary message through Elijah was to show Israel's God could powerfully provide what Baal couldn't for this poor widow—food. She expected to die along with her son. Yet the living God saved her life, and twice, the life of her son.

Apparently, this widow was not a believer in Jehovah, but Elijah had promised she would be taken care of. We wouldn't expect her to believe him, yet she did. She risked a lot to obey a foreigner. What would her neighbors think? Would her god Baal punish her? Of course, she was already in danger of dying, but now, she risked being seen as a fool. What kind of smart Sidon woman would fall for such a lie from a person who believed in a false God—Jehovah—even if he was a self-proclaimed prophet.

Then the worst thing happens. Her son, who was earlier spared from death, suddenly dies. Jehovah, who she had begun trusting, has failed her. Will she return to her old god or seek her new God? She was raised to worship and trust in gods like Baal who supposedly could raise the dead. Yet because of her previous encounter with Elijah, she didn't go to Baal to ask for her son's healing, she went to Elijah. What a wonderful baby step of faith. God healed her son through Elijah, and her faith became secure in Jehovah.

Whenever we read the accounts in the Old Testament, we should be thinking in terms of the ways Jesus is referenced even in subtle ways. In this story of a Gentile woman's needs being met, we see how God is pointing to the future when the gospel will be preached to both Jew and Gentile (Romans 3:29).

4. Sometimes when we serve others in obedience to God, we assume we will be protected from unfortunate challenges or experiences. Do you think that assumption is correct or false? Explain.

   A. Can you think of any other incorrect assumption people have because they are serving God or others?

   B. How or why do you think people begin to accept such a wrong assumption?

C. Romans 8:28 and James 1:2–4 are verses which counteract this assumption. Can you think of others?

Many people believe if they become a Christian, their life will have no problems. Of course, God does promise abundant life (John 10:10), but he didn't mean a perfect, stress-free life. We should never look at only one verse and make conclusions. We need to study all the Bible to form beliefs consistent with it all. Other Scripture passages teach an abundant life might not align with what our human nature longs for: no problems, quick solutions, and the ability to be perfect. If we lived a problem–free life, we wouldn't need God. God allows our challenges to teach us to depend upon him more and more.

For additional study, go to: Exodus 23:29–30, Matthew 26:41, John 16:33, Acts 14:22, Romans 8:35, Romans 12:12, 1 Corinthians 10:13, and Revelation 2:9–10.

5. Read 2 Kings 4:1–7.

   A. What were this widow's beliefs about her resources (v. 2)?

   B. How was the widow required to increase her resources and what boldness did that require?

C. How do people have similar attitudes about their abilities to courageously obey God in service to others?

D. How do you think she fearlessly represented God to her world?

Here we have another example of a needy widow. God must be communicating to us he will provide for the lowest and most disadvantaged people by giving them strength to trust him. No one can say anything like, "I don't have the resources others do. God can't help or empower me. I'm disadvantaged."

The fact this widow was married to a prophet emphasizes serving God doesn't always guarantee life without struggles. For whatever reason, this family was in debt when the prophet died. Either this family spent money frivolously or they were wise, but circumstances overwhelmed their resources. The Jewish law provided for debts to be paid off by a family member becoming a servant with parameters of how long the service would last. God is not heartless. Ultimately, every indentured servant was released at the year of jubilee (every fifty years).

Did this widow need God's courage to humble herself to ask her neighbors to borrow their jars and vessels? God could have directed Elisha to snap his fingers and create oil in abundance or hand her cash. But in this case, God wanted the widow to be involved. Did she need to feel included? Was her grief overwhelming her? Was she disheartened because of past harsh treatment? We don't know. Regardless, God knew what she needed to prompt her to act.

Interestingly, she says, "Your servant has nothing in the house except a jar of oil." When we are overwhelmed, and especially when we're depressed or discouraged, we might focus on what we don't have rather than on what we do have—even if it's a little jar of oil. She does acknowledge the jar, so good for her. God takes her little and makes it big. We also can confidently surrender to God's plan even if our victorious step feels very small.

We also see the woman didn't know the complete plan. Elisha gave her one part of the plan but not the rest. The widow had to be resolute in following through. She saw God work and God received the credit, not Elisha. Once she completed the first task, she asked Elisha what was next. Whether or not she could guess, we don't know. Regardless, she wasn't careless but asked for further direction.

As trusting Christians, we should take one step at a time and then wait to see how God leads further. His direction may not come quickly. When God doesn't give us the whole plan, we must be careful to take the first step, even when we're walking into a fog. God is faithful. He will "part" the fog and guide us.

6. Like the widow's experience, sometimes God asks us to step out in faith stretching our confidence. Have you ever experienced that? What happened?

A. Later, did you wonder why you hadn't stepped out before?

B. How did your faith or courage grow?

C. How were other people influenced?

7. Scan 2 Kings 4:8–37.

   A. How does this woman of Shunem show a courageous, spiritual sensitivity her husband may lack (v. 9)?

   B. How did this woman show generosity (v. 10)?

   C. When the woman of Shunem is given the promise of a son, how does she respond (v. 16) and what do you think her response reveals?

   D. How does verse 28 give some possible insight into her hesitant thinking?

E. What curious things happen in this passage?

F. If you could speak to this woman, what would you ask her about her courage?

G. What are your thoughts about her husband?

Elisha told Gehazi in verse 29 to lay Elisha's staff upon the boy's face. The staff represented Elisha's God-given power. Putting it there before Elisha could arrive meant this child "belonged" to Elisha and nothing could attack him. (For deeper study, look at Exodus 4:1–4 and 17:8–13).

8. Have you ever lacked the courage to ask God for something you want? Why?

   A. Can you remember a time you initially hesitated and then asked God? What happened?

   B. If you've had an opportunity to encourage someone to ask God for something, what did you say? What Scripture did you use?

We are studying two needy women, one a Gentile and one a Jew, who took care of Elijah and Elisha. God provided for both. God is communicating no one is unimportant to him. Such a wonderful truth is even more striking when we remember women were not valued in Middle Eastern cultures. With some men, women were merely an object who provided needed tasks, including producing an heir. There must have been times God led Elijah and Elisha to help men, but God chose to often highlight how he helped women.

The woman who lived in Zarephath was a foreigner, but this widow of a prophet is an Israelite, living in the territory of Issachar, who was one of the twelve sons of Jacob. Again, God is pointing our attention to his desire to express his love for everyone, both Jews and Gentiles. Jesus will stress many years later he came to save both Jews and Gentiles—something the Jews never would have anticipated (Romans 3:29).

We don't know the reasons this woman didn't boldly ask Elisha to help her seek God for the child she wanted. Second Kings 4:28 might give some insight into a possible mixed motive. She could be afraid if she did ask, her desires wouldn't be granted, and she would feel like she had been deceived. She would rather avoid disappointment than fearlessly believe God knew what was best for her.

Our motives can easily be mixed. In fact, no one acts with pure motives—otherwise, we would be perfect. Only Jesus had a singular motive and unflinchingly followed through on it—to obey his Father and make sure his plan was fulfilled.

We can easily be like this woman. Protecting ourselves from being deceived and disappointed certainly are only two possible reasons. We might not go to God for other reasons. Maybe we feel unworthy. Maybe we have experienced so much rejection in our lives we can't imagine someone giving us what we want. Maybe we believe God is like a mean person who delights in withholding our desires from us.

But God wants to provide courage to overcome our fears and trust him with our desires. We can ask ourselves, "Am I willing to ask and trust God knows what is best, even if it's 'no'?"

Evaluating our motives is very important because then we'll be able to identify how we are obstructed from believing God's promises. Correcting those lies will give us bold assurance to serve selflessly.

9. Read 2 Kings 5:1–3.

   A. What wrong reaction to her slavery did this young girl resist?

   B. In what way(s) did she show a servant's heart and genuine love?

   C. How do you think she was able to put aside fear in order to be courageous in speaking up?

   D. As a result of her courageous faith, how did she influence her world (2 Kings 5:14-15)?

10. Read Mark 12:41–44.

    A. What character quality did Jesus call attention to in this woman's service?

    B. Why did it take courage to do what she did?

    C. What kind of influence do you think she had on her world?

    D. Why do you think she was willing to be anonymous?

    E. How does her anonymity speak to you?

    F. Do you relate to any of the fears this woman must have overcome to be sacrificial?

11. Tithing and giving money for God's Kingdom is one important way of serving him. What principles or attitudes about godly giving are encouraged in the following verses from 2 Corinthians 8 and 9?

Verse	Principles
8:1–5	
8:8	
8:9	
8:14	
9:6	
9:7	
9:8	
9:9–10	
9:11–12	
9:13	
9:14	

A. Which of the verses are most meaningful to you?

B. Does any one of the verses or principles indicate you should make a difference in your finances or giving?

C. What kind of courage will you need to make any changes?

12. Read Luke 5:15–16.

    A, Why do you think some women feel guilty if they aren't serving every moment?

    B. When Jesus left the needy, what do you think those left behind might have thought?

    C. If you don't constantly serve, what might you be afraid of hearing from others? Or what do you fear they will think about you?

D. How does the choice Jesus made instruct, inspire, or encourage you?

13. Read Matthew 20:28.

    A. How do you think Jesus's understanding of his own identity and mission give him courage to serve?

    B. Do you have an awareness of your identity as a daughter of the King—a princess? How would you describe it?

    C. Does that give you courage in any way?

14. How do you think God is guiding you based on this lesson?

15. Was there anything new or important for you in this lesson?

Serving is more complicated than we think. There are so many ways to serve God and each one takes a particular kind of courage energized by God.

Women in particular think they need to serve everyone and at every opportunity. We falsely believe saying "no" to anything is a lack of courage. But God gives different responsibilities based on his fulfillment of his kingdom. The wise and courageous woman remembers to check with God's leading before committing to serving. An opportunity is not necessarily God's open door.

My Precious Princess and Daughter:

You can change your world through my power. You are a woman of influence because you represent me.

Of course, you want to be appreciated. I will cause your service to be acknowledged at the right time. Welcome the positive comments from others. I want your heart to be encouraged. But don't worship the applause. You can trust my accolades will be even more valuable in heaven.

Resist discouragement when you encounter difficult challenges while serving. My enemy tells you service will protect you from opposition. But I will use the obstacles to purify and strengthen you.

My daughter, seek my balance of prayer, rest, and service. Because you hear of a need or are asked to help doesn't necessarily mean I'm calling you to respond to that invitation. Seek my guidance. You'll be set free from the paralyzing hold of people-pleasing. I know that's best for you.

Be assured, I'm using you according to the plan I have for you and only intend it for your good.

Lovingly,
Your Heavenly Father, the King

~Lesson 3~
Courageously Overcoming Discouragement

Have you noticed the word "courage" in the word discouragement? Makes sense, right? Discouragement is the "dis" of courage, the lack of courage. When we are discouraged, we lack emotional, mental, and spiritual strength. We are easily intimidated, swayed from our convictions, and focused more on the negative.

We need courage to fight discouragement. Only God can provide what we lack. Our Heavenly Father delights to come through for us. God desires to empower us to fight the overwhelming feelings. He will reveal why we are held back from obeying him. When he strengthens us with courage, regardless of the forces against us, he is motivated by two main reasons: he wants the best for us, and his empowering gives himself glory in the eyes of others. No wonder he wants to lavish us with his courage, which he has in abundance.

Many things and experiences can contribute to discouragement. No one is exempt. Let's see together how we can battle victoriously against this bitter aspect of life which sucks the joy out of our perspective and responses.

1. What causes discouragement in you most often?

A. How do you overcome these feelings?

B. What encourages you to fight?

C. What synonyms would you use to describe your feelings and mental state when you lack courage?

D. Can you envision any metaphor or visual picture to describe discouragement?

2. Look at the lives of the following biblical women and identify what was causing their discouragement and how they overcame it.

Verse	Name	Situation	Her solution
Mark 5:25–34			
Mark 7:24–30; Matthew 15:21–28			
Luke 13:11–13			
John 8:1–11			

A. How do you think these women influenced others after their encounter with Jesus?

B. What would have given them the boldness to talk about Jesus with others?

C. What might each one focus on from their encounter, aiding them in fighting discouragement in the future?

D. Can you relate to any of these women, whether you have experienced exactly the same situation? Explain.

The story of Jesus's interaction with the Syrophoenician woman (Mark 7:24–30; Matthew 15:21–28) can be hard to understand. We perceive Jesus as mean and unloving, wanting to destroy her courage. We would expect he would be more encouraging and use gentle words with a Gentile, because he wanted to share the good news of why he was on earth. This exchange doesn't make sense—until we understand Jesus's motive and the message he wanted to convey.

This Gentile woman must have arrived at this home discouraged as she sought help for her precious struggling daughter (7:25). She fell at his feet. We can only suspect she had tried to find help from every avenue with no success.

Then she heard about Jesus and his reputation. She must try this one last hope. She begged him (v. 26). In spite of her strong personality, her self-reliance was being stretched to the breaking point. She became convinced she was no longer in control. From our viewpoint, Jesus's words must lead her into the valley of hopelessness.

Then Jesus told her, "Let the children be fed first, for it is not right to take the children's bread and throw it to the dogs" (Mark 7:27). Jesus had a specific reason for saying this to her.

His words were more a metaphor than referring to a family dinner. The "children" were symbolically the Jews, the "children" in God's family. The "dogs" were anyone not in the "family;" therefore, the Gentiles. Jews considered the Gentiles unclean like the dogs running loose in the streets. No one took in a dog for a pet. Dogs survived by eating whatever they could find, including filth. Jesus was indeed saying the worst possible thing he could about her.

But notice her reply. The rest of us might cower in fear, even run away feeling rejected. Or we might become defensive, loudly telling everyone he can't be the Messiah, he's so uncouth. To try to regain some element of self-respect, we might gossip about him to anyone who would listen. *I'll show him he can't treat me like that.*

Not her. "Yes, Lord; yet even the dogs under the table eat the children's crumbs" (v. 28). What courage. What strength. Jesus had to be chuckling under his breath, because he expected this kind of spunk from her. He wanted her to see the strength of her faith in him for her encouragement. She had no trouble acknowledging Jesus's priority was to minister to his own people, and she would settle for crumbs. He would still have more than sufficient power left for healing her daughter.

Yes, there was a sense Jesus was putting her in her place. He wanted her to come to the end of her self-sufficiency and depend upon him. With Jesus's final rebuff, she was ready to admit her neediness and put her faith in him. Jesus affirmed her, "great is your faith" (Matthew 15:28). Her daughter was healed.

We must also wonder if this encounter was preparing Jesus's disciples and the others who were watching as Jesus again granted a non-Jew what they desired. His followers' emotions and minds would be fighting against this anti-Jewish thinking. They have no idea someday they would preach the Gospel to "the other side of the tracks" and welcome Gentiles into the newly formed church. When that happened, did they remember this encounter? Maybe they thought, "No wonder Jesus healed that Gentile woman's daughter. He was preparing us even then."

When we look at how Jesus responded to each person he encountered on earth, we notice each response was unique. He responded according to the needs of each one. He intimately knew their motives for approaching him. Each individual was convinced they knew what they needed, but only Jesus could accurately understand what was best for each life. His response wasn't only about providing for their need but growing their faith and dependence on him. He wanted to dispel their self-sufficiency, or whatever else blocked them from surrendering themselves to him as Savior and Lord.

Jesus wasn't mean to this woman. He offered her a unique gift intended specifically for her good.

3. How might the following verses give you insights for fighting discouragement with perseverance?

A. John 15:4–6:

B. Romans 15:4:

C. Ephesians 6:18:

D. II Timothy 1:12:

E. II Timothy 4:7–8:

4. In what ways does II Timothy 4:2 give confidence for courageous perseverance about impacting others?

The Bible is God's gift of encouragement by including both instruction and stories of real people. One such narrative is the book of Ruth, which includes the heartbreak that two women, Ruth and Naomi, experience deeply and how God empowers them to trust him.

5. Scan the book of Ruth.

A. Why was Naomi discouraged (1:3, 5)?

B. Although God does allow calamity in our lives (Isaiah 45:6–7), what incorrect attitude contributed to Naomi's discouragement (vss. 20–21)?

C. What good things in her life did Naomi disregard and how did her choices fuel her discouragement (1:10, 14, 16–17)?

6. How did God encourage Naomi and Ruth?

   A. 2:3:

   B. 2:8–9:

   C. 2:11:

D. 4:1–6:

E. 4:13:

F. 4:17:

The book of Ruth is a powerhouse story of humanity's emotional struggles and God's gracious provision. We are carried along by the story of grief and abandonment. Certainly, Naomi had every reason to grieve. She was now a widow and childless. She had two daughters-in-law who loved her, but in that culture, females didn't have much power and certainly no earning power. No wonder Naomi felt overwhelmed. She literally did not know where her next meal would come from and how she would be protected from men who took advantage of needy widows. Sons were the only source a widow had to provide for her and protect her. And she had none. Now she would be responsible for Ruth and Orpah. No wonder she urged them to return to their childhood homes, the only place where they could be cared for and remarry.

Even in her depression and discouragement, God was unconditionally gracious. He didn't forsake her even though she discounted him as a possible sustainer. Even worse she misrepresented God's nature by blaming him (1:13, 20–21). God didn't cut her off but instead, through amazing and creative circumstances, he provided all she and a Gentile daughter-in-law needed.

As the story unfolds, we can feel Naomi's spirits lifting. Her eyes were more open to the possibility God's hand was upon them. Her courage increased, and she had the wisdom to tell Ruth how to proceed to make herself available to Boaz.

One of the characteristics of discouragement is refusing to believe anything good can happen. God's care for Naomi and Ruth can encourage any of us who are emotionally struggling. He never gives up and never casts off his children—you and me—no matter how hard it is for us to think rightly about him.

7. Sometimes misunderstanding who God is or the way he works destroys courage. How do the following verses describe God's nature? Also include the lie that opposes the truth of who he is, even if it's not mentioned in the verse(s).

   A. Numbers 23:19:

   B. I Chronicles 29:11–12:

   C. Psalm 18:30:

   D. Psalm 99:1, 9:

E. Lamentations 3:22–23:

F. Isaiah 55:7–9:

G. Matthew 11:28–30:

H. Ephesians 1:18–20:

I. James 1:5:

J. Revelation 15:3–4:

8. Which of God's qualities help you most strongly fight against discouragement? Explain.

9. What lie about God's qualities sometimes disheartens you?

Knowing accurately God's attributes can mean all the difference in fighting discouragement. If as believers in God and his Son we are basing our outlook with an accurate perspective of God, we have a solid foundation for faith. But if we believe in ideas about a god other than who the Almighty God of the universe really is, we have every reason to be discouraged.

Think of it this way. If we think God is weak, a liar, doesn't keep his promises, is selfish, needy, stupid, confused, powerless, imperfect, and mean, is there any hope? No. Is there any solid foundation? No. Of course, all of us would say, "But I don't think of him that way."

Whether or not we think of his qualities truthfully is revealed by the choices we make in each challenge or joy of life. In many ways, we behave and make decisions as if his character is based on lies. Especially when we experience risk, the truths about his nature aren't on our minds, and our heart responds like we believe the lies.

If we could be perfect on this earth everything would be different. We would instantly evaluate the beliefs of our inner heart and replace the lies with the truth of his character. Then we would never respond in any sinful way. We would always trust in a God who is completely good, kind, loving, wise, patient, and faithful, and who also hates and is wrathful against sin because of its damage to his creation and created ones.

Thank God, he doesn't expect perfection of any of us. Instead, he longs for us to grow in our confidence in the truth of who he is and then act courageously because we trust in his holy characteristics.

10. Pick one of the characteristics in the following paragraph describing God, written by Adam Clarke (1762-1832), a British Methodist theologian. Concentrate on it this week.

> [God is] the eternal, independent, and self-existent Being; the Being whose purposes and actions spring from himself, without foreign motive or influence; he who is absolute in dominion; the most pure, the most simple, the most spiritual of all essences; infinitely perfect; and eternally self-sufficient, needing nothing that he has made; illimitable in his immensity, inconceivable in his mode of existence, and indescribable in his essence; known fully only by himself, because infinite mind can only be fully comprehended by itself. In a word, a Being who, from his infinite wisdom, cannot err or be deceived, and from his infinite goodness, can do nothing but what is eternally just, and right, and kind.[1]

A. Scan through Psalm 103 and check off the above list (Adam Clarke's list) any of God's characteristics the psalmist includes. As you continue to study the Bible, notice when God's qualities are mentioned. You might want to begin developing your own list of those qualities.

B. What reactions (e.g., worry, discontent, bitterness, hatred, lack of self-control, etc.) reveal you may not be trusting in the truths about God as much as you thought?

C. What godly choices (e.g., love, joy, peace, kindness, self-control, wisdom, etc.) are you making that reveal you are believing truths about God?

11. Is there anything you need to change in your perspective of God based on insights from this lesson?

All the characteristics of God are revealed in Jesus, who is God incarnate. If we want to see God's qualities in action, we only need to read the Gospel accounts (Matthew, Mark, Luke, and John) of Jesus's life on earth.

12. Read Matthew 26:36–46.

A. How would you describe Jesus's state of mind and heart at this point?

B. What are your feelings and thoughts as you are reminded of Jesus in this state?

C. How does this story impact you for challenging times?

God-in-the-flesh Jesus, Almighty God, arrived on earth wrapped in human flesh with human emotions. Even though he was God, he didn't escape the challenges of humanity. He felt discouraged, he was tempted, rejected, spurned, misunderstood, and lied about—far more than any of us have ever experienced.

In light of that, pause and think of Jesus's determination to die for our sins. He was undaunted, fulfilling his Father's plan at every cost to himself. He wasn't like the other people who died on crosses. Every crucified man had committed sins, even if their sins weren't the ones they were being killed for. The two men crucified alongside Jesus deserved condemnation for the sins they'd committed. But Jesus was the only human ever on earth who never committed a single sin and was falsely accused and died completely innocent. Plus, he had the power to remove himself from the cross.

Yet he voluntarily remained on the cross and took on every sin every human had chosen and ever would choose. But the most agonizing part was how those sins caused separation from his holy Heavenly Father—a horrible spiritual distance when previously they had always enjoyed total oneness and pure connection.

To please his Father, he courageously endured the agony of torture even as he cared for others like Peter and his mother. Then he surrendered to death and three days later, victoriously arose from the grave—all in accordance with his Father's plan, fashioned from before the earth was created.

Our confident courage can spring from that sprouting seed of God's plan spreading across the earth. Satan and his forces are determined to destroy the message of salvation. Yet the gospel continues to be spread and to transform lives. How glorious.

If you haven't yet acknowledged how your self-sufficiency has failed you, nor have you recognized your determination to earn your way into heaven through good works, I have good news for you. Jesus's death and resurrection makes it possible for you to receive eternal life without achieving a certain level of goodness. We all stand equally guilty at the cross of Christ and yet can be assured we are forgiven and cleansed and will be welcomed into heaven because of Jesus's sacrificial gift. There are no essential words you need say. God knows your heart. Tell him you need him because you have sinned. Your acknowledgment might take courage but ask God for that courage also. He will give it.

If you made that decision, please attend a local church. I'd also love to hear from you at www.KathyCollardMiller.com

May Ephesians 1:19–20 empower all of us with courage beyond our own capabilities because our courage is from God:

> And what is the immeasurable greatness of his power toward us who believe, according to the working of his great might that he worked in Christ when he raised him from the dead and seated him at his right hand in the heavenly places.

My Precious Princess and Daughter:

My love for you is so great, you will spend the rest of your life trying to comprehend it. I want you to be encouraged by my unconditional love for you. You'll never come to the end of my love for you—it's that bountiful. When you're discouraged, keep your eyes on me and my committed love for you.

When it feels like life isn't worth living, remember who I am. I never change. I am faithful. I am always aware of everything going on in your life. I am involved in every aspect of your life. I stand ready to provide you with everything you need. I never sleep, and I never take a vacation. That's why you can rest, relax, trust, and obey. Abide in me and don't worry about the difficulties facing you. I'm in charge.

When you know you've failed ... when you see those you love in trouble ... when your dreams fall through, and you must find new ones ... look to me. Don't let my enemy keep your eyes on the disappointment and discouraging feelings. Focus on my promises and who I am.

I am your Father. I love you. I am worthy of your trust.
Lovingly,
Your Heavenly Father, the King

~Lesson 4~
Courageous Within My Family

Families can often be our greatest joy, yet also our greatest sorrow. The first couple, Adam and Eve, chose sinfully even though they lived in God's perfect creation. Then their first child, a son, chose to murder his brother rather than humbly please God. Obviously, perfect and near perfect surroundings didn't result in perfect godly choices. And our current world is even farther from any hint of perfection.

No wonder we need God's courage and strength to wisely love family members. Those we love can easily become more important than God and his godly ways. We desperately need to know God's direction and commit to the belief he knows the better way.

In this lesson, we will see how God wants to empower us to love our family according to his wise perspective. We aren't surprised only he has the perfect plan because he created mankind.

1. In what ways do you think you need courage for any relationship challenges within your family?

A. What do you enjoy most about being part of a family?

B. What is your greatest struggle being a part of a family?

2. Read Genesis 2:18–23.

    A. Why did God create a family (vs. 18)?

    B. Why do you think God gave Adam the responsibilities of working the land and naming the animals before revealing he intended to provide a unique companion for Adam (vv. 15, 19–20)?

    C. What need within Adam do you think naming the animals provided?

    D. To what extent do you think Adam thought the animals would meet his emotional needs?

E. Why did God do so much to prepare Adam to see his need of a human companion?

God knew all along he would create Eve. Yet he first gave Adam purpose through naming the animals and working the land. Interestingly, verse 18 says before Adam named the animals, God said (to himself), "It is not good that the man should be alone; I will make him a helper fit for him." Then he gave Adam the assignment of naming the animals. We can easily wonder if Adam thought working the land and being involved with the animals might be his total responsibilities and all he needed.

Adam must have noticed the animals came in pairs. But there was no "pair" for him. God was really stoking Adam's healthy desires. Did Adam wonder if he was missing out? God made sure Adam first saw everything around him as insufficient and unsatisfying before bringing Adam's perfect companion onto the scene.

Naming the animals suggested Adam had authority over them. Yet even though Adam named Eve, they were co-laborers, not the man being "over" her like he was with the animals. Man is created for relationship—both with God and with other people. Animals were not created for the purpose of relationship but as support for mankind.

Looking again at Genesis 2:18, God uses the Hebrew word for "fit" suggesting synonyms like, "corresponding to, likened to, adapted to, counterpart." We could say, "a helper matching him."

We might wonder whether God's plan to make Adam hunger for someone who is his pair should have motivated him to be more gracious with his imperfect match. Often, we become dissatisfied with our family members and think we would be better without them. When we feel discouraged, ready to divorce ourselves emotionally or legally, we can remind ourselves of the loneliness without a family member—even if imperfect. If God has designed for a person to be married or have a particular family member, we can remember, "it is not good that the man [or any person] should be alone."

3. Read Genesis 2:24–25.

   A. What principle for marriage and family does Genesis 2:24 give?

   B. Since extended families have lived together throughout history, do you think physical or emotional cleaving is being considered here? Explain.

   C. What difficulties occur when one of the married partners doesn't emotionally separate from a parent?

   D. How would you describe your separating process from your parents and family members after your wedding? If you are not married, what do you think it should be like?

E. If a family member encourages you to put your original family before the needs or ideas of your husband, how would Genesis 2:24 give you courage to make your husband your priority?

Staying emotionally dependent upon a parent or other family member creates problems in a marriage. A person can physically move out of their childhood home, but their heart—their commitment and loyalty—can be with their parents or other family members. Maybe a wife doesn't have the courage to believe God can provide for her needs, so she seeks the opinions of a family member, while discounting her husband's ideas.

Or maybe she doesn't have the courage to believe God will provide for her own parents. She believes she must continue to be involved in their lives, fearing they can't do without her. Her husband becomes secondary in importance.

Being separated from everything we know and love, and beginning a new family, requires trust in God. We must recognize God is our primary source and provides power to focus on our husband.

4. Why do you think God included in the account the fact Adam and Eve were naked yet unashamed (vs. 25)?

Genesis 2:25 portrays the ideal innocence God intended for marriage. There was no speck of discomfort between them. They were completely innocent.

A total absence of shame indicates they didn't know what sin or guilt was. So far nothing wrong had been done. They trusted God implicitly. They didn't know what they didn't know. There was nothing suggesting the world could be any other way. They needed no courage to live in complete happiness and assurance of God's goodness.

God's formation of this marriage between Adam and Eve and the expectation of a coming family from their union, is a type and shadow of the eternal family of God. The Bible is filled with spiritual concepts, and this is one of the many. The depiction of Adam and Eve's perfect innocence points to the future freedom from sin for God's children in heaven. We will be spiritually naked and unafraid.

Today when we have a spiritual hunger for the freedom of a sinless world, we often say, "we want to return to the Garden of Eden." Likewise, as God developed within Adam a hunger for a match, he develops within us a desire for the heavenly perfection. We can have courage knowing God has the perfect plan.

5. Read Genesis 3:1–7.

   A. What disrupts the innocence and purity of the Garden?

   B. What is most important to you about how the "first couple" are affected by their sin?

C. How does Genesis 3:7 contrast with Genesis 2:25?

D. What does the phrase "eyes of both were opened" mean to you in practical or daily ways?

Although Adam and Eve did not take hold of God's courage to resist Satan's temptation, we can grow stronger to identify the lies of temptation. We will study the topic of temptation at great length in Lesson 9 of this book.

6. What significant promise does God make in Genesis 3:15?

   A. Write Genesis 3:15 in your own words.

   B. Does recognizing how God points to the promise of future spiritual deliverance immediately after the first sin give you courage for your present life? Explain your answer.

Although this verse can appear very confusing, remember God is speaking to Satan. When God says, "he shall bruise your head," read it this way: "my Messiah will destroy you by bruising your head—a death blow against your power." When God follows it with, "and you shall bruise his heel," God is saying, "you will bruise my Messiah's heel through his death on the cross, but it will not be a death blow."

When life delivers a death blow, we can have courage knowing God will walk with us through the challenge. Stumbling in our walk with God doesn't take away our salvation or our right to enter heaven. Sinning, doubting, or making an unwise choice is a "bruise" to our "heel," not to our "head." Such truths empower our perseverance. We know God has the final victory.

7. Scan Genesis 4:1–16.

   A. What is your reaction to how sin continued quickly through Cain?

   B. What do you think made Cain angry (vs. 4–6)?

   C. Both sons offered sacrifices to God. Why do you think one way was acceptable and the other not?

   D. In what way would you say Cain lacked courage in his reactions to God and his brother?

E. What advice would you give Cain?

F. Is there anything meaningful to you about how God tried to reason with Cain (vss. 6–7)?

G. What lies about God do you think Cain was believing?

Some commentators believe Eve thought Cain, her first born, was the promised one who would "bruise" the head of Satan (Genesis 3:15). After all, she exclaimed, "I have gotten a man with the help of the Lord" (4:1). Eve's declaration could indicate she took some credit for the provision—and of course, she was involved. Little did she know the real fulfillment, Messiah Jesus, wouldn't arrive on the scene until thousands of years later through a humble virgin.

Eve's misunderstanding could represent two primary ways people regard salvation. One view declares, "I'll save myself by being good enough." The other says, "I can't save myself no matter how good I am. I need to acknowledge only Jesus's finished work on the cross can save me."

Those two views are contrasted in the sacrifices Cain and Abel offered to God. Cain's offering was not acceptable, but Abel's offering was. We don't have a record of how Cain and Abel knew what was acceptable to God. Yet God held them accountable so they must have known. God tries to reason with Cain to bring him to repentance, but Cain cared more about his pride and selfishness. Although we can only guess what lies Cain believed about God, they must be like the lies fueling our disobedience and distrust:

- God isn't good; he has disappointed me.
- God doesn't want my best; I know what is best.
- God should let me do whatever I want to do; he doesn't understand my pain.
- God won't provide for me; he didn't in the past.

The list goes on and on. The lies about life, the world, people, and how I can be happy are the lies formed early in life. We must ask God for his courage to risk admitting he knows better.

As the narrative continues about Adam and Eve's descendants, God emphasizes how quickly humanity's sinful choices impact all of life—even to the point of murder. After all, if some descendants of the first couple lived without sin and only over time chose ungodly reactions here and there, we could believe a viewpoint like, "Well, it's only because of increasing temptation from the stresses of civilization that people sin more and more. Every person has a pure heart. Everyone is a good person. Life makes it hard to stay pure and good. You just have to try the best you can."

The fact total depravity continues with the first-born child reveals the truth every person is born with a sinful nature. Sin has nothing to do with circumstances or the corruption of the world. The corruption of the world is a result of the sinful choices of humankind. No wonder we need God's provision of courage and strength to fight against our sinful human tendencies.

8. Read Genesis 25:19–34.

   A. What problems did this family struggle with?

   B. How did Rebekah and Isaac influence their family negatively (v. 28)?

   C. How do you think Rebekah lacked courage to trust and obey God (Genesis 27:5–13)? To what degree did her husband's actions play into that, do you think?

   D. What consequences does Rebekah pay for her deceit and lack of spiritual strength (Genesis 28:7–9)?

   E. What fact(s) about God do you think Rebekah believed?

F. How does believing lies about God diminish your courageous perseverance to obey him?

G. Have you ever had an experience where God's work was blocked—according to your understanding—by the choices of someone else? How did you handle it? To what degree did you need courage?

Some commentators believe Rebekah's barrenness lasted for twenty years because Isaac was sixty years old when Rebekah became pregnant (25:26). We can certainly understand how the delay could erode Rebekah's trust in God. When God did fulfill her desire, she could be afraid God's promise of Jacob gaining the inheritance would not be accomplished because her husband, Isaac, wasn't cooperating with God's plan. He wanted to give the inheritance to Esau, not the one chosen by God, Jacob.

When God disappoints us through some delay, or a "no" to our desires, we can struggle but God doesn't condemn us. He offers strength to persist with courageous trust in him. The story of Rebekah can be both a warning and an encouragement to persevere.

Rebekah made a curious statement when the twins "struggled within her." She said, "If it is thus, why is this happening to me?" (Genesis 25:22). Sometimes we say similar things: "God gave me the answer to my prayer, so I thought things would go smoothly now." A wife whose husband becomes a believer may wonder why he is still prone to the things that aggravated her in the beginning.

A woman might pray for her dismissive boss to be replaced and when her friend is placed in the position, her friend becomes an obstacle to her goals. A barren woman might pray to conceive but when she does, she miscarries.

So often we think answers to prayer mean smooth sailing. But God doesn't guarantee that. The strength to trust God despite obstacles requires believing God's motive is always for our good.

9. Look at the verses below. What courage did each woman need? If you faced that challenge, what truth would give you courage?

Verses	Woman	Needed Courage	Truth
Numbers 27:1–7			
Judges 13:2–25			
I Samuel 1:1–28			
II Chronicles 22:10–12, 23:11			
Luke 1:26–38			
Acts 16:1; II Timothy 1:2–5			

A. List two or three truths you can draw from the lives of these women.

B. How do you want to apply those truths to be more courageous within your marriage and family?

10. Read Mark 3:20–21; 31–35.

    A. Why do you think the opinions of Jesus's family did not diminish his courage to fulfill his Father's plan for him?

    B. What are the opinions of you by your family members that have diminished or attempted to diminish your courage?

    C. How did you respond? Did you reflect upon any Scripture? Did Jesus's example help you?

11. As you think of what you've learned in this lesson, in what one area would you like to increase your courage to trust and obey God?

    A. What are some possible obstacles you might face?

    B. What kind of courage does God want to provide? If possible, share a truth from Scripture.

As we've studied the biblical recounting of dysfunctional marriages and families, God emphasizes our need of his courageous power.

God's creation of Adam and Eve detail God's plan for marriage. The sad accounting of Cain and Abel points us to recognize how familial relationships must be protected. The control issues of Rebekah remind us we can trust God to fulfill his will. In the lives of biblical characters, we often see the root of making people and family a higher priority than God.

That's why the Bible encourages us to take a hold of God's boldness to believe he knows the best way—other people including family do not. Our gracious God offers us a little push of courage toward trusting him more by assuring us earth cannot meet our needs. Only the perfections of heaven can do that where our "marriage" with Jesus our King will be for a perfect eternity.

My Precious Princess and Daughter:

You are one of my children, and I have given you a courageous heart. Facing and acknowledging the ways you sinfully turn from me will strengthen you to trust me more and more. As I forgive and cleanse you, you will know that you can always trust my unconditional love.

I wasn't shocked or surprised when Adam and Eve sinned amidst the perfection of my garden. I'm not shocked or surprised when you falter, struggle, or lack courage. I already knew my plan to restore humanity's fellowship with me, and I already know how I'll strengthen you to persevere in trusting me.

I included specific family stories in my Word to let you know you are not alone. There is nothing too hard for me. I am never caught off guard. I will guide you.

I understand your desire for your family's happiness. You may think you know best but trust me as the one who has the power to make changes.

As you reach out to others, be gentle. If someone isn't responding the way you'd like, I understand your frustration. But it's not your job to change them. Only I can work within a person's heart. You can't be their god.

Receive my power to become the courageous woman you want to be, and I want to empower you to be.

Let others see me working in your life. Relax and trust me for my Spirit's work in another person's life.

Lovingly,
Your Heavenly Father, the King

~Lesson 5~
Courageous in My Church

Gaining courage from being with other Christians can be described as a group of burning logs glowing brightly. But if one log is removed to sit out in the cold by itself, its glow will wither; its flame will die out. We need fellowship with other Christians to maintain our courage, and they need us for the vibrant life of the body of Christ.

Yet, let's be honest, the church is filled with other people like us: imperfect, struggling, and selfish, who don't always trust God. At times, there's more discouragement than encouragement from interacting with our brothers and sisters in Christ. Regardless, God calls for us to meet together. How can he expect us to thrive amid such imperfections?

Indeed, he expects exactly that. Let's see how his Word directs us to grow in courage as we see the importance of the body of Christ.

1. As you think of the concept of "church," answer these questions.

    A. What do you think is God's intended purpose of the concept of church?

B. If you attend church, what do you like best about it?

C. If you don't attend church, what prevents you from going?

D. If you had hurtful experiences from some group of Christians, what happened and what was most hurtful about it?

E. If something were different at another church that would overcome your hesitation about attending, what is that difference?

2. Courageous women were involved at the beginning of the formation of the church. Chart here those women and their roles (if one is mentioned).

Verse(s)	Name	What occurred or involvement
Acts 1:12–14		
Acts 9:36–42		

Acts 16:13–15		
Acts 18:24–26; Romans 16:3–5		
Romans 16:1–2		
Romans 16:6, 12, 15		

A. Are any of these women and their role an example to you? Whose and why?

B. Are you surprised to see so many women mentioned in Scripture? Explain your answer.

C. Do you think women required more courage at the time of the early church to follow Christ than a man? Or no difference? Explain your answer.

D. Do you think it takes more courage now, at this point in history, for a woman or a man to follow Christ? Or no difference? Explain your answer.

3. The early church, including the women mentioned above, suffered persecution, which required courage. What characteristics of courage marked the early church as described in these verses from Acts?

   A. 1:14:

   B. 2:42–43:

   C. 2:44–45:

   D. 2:46–47:

   E. 4:1–4, 8, 13:

   F. 4:18–20:

   G. 4:23–31:

H. 4:32–37:

I. 5:1–11:

J. 6:1–7:

4. In what ways do you think the early church needed courage?

5. Which of those characteristics are reasonable expectations for today's church?

Although it was good news, because the number of those involved in the young church was increasing, it soon became evident not everything was perfect. There were unaddressed needs and discontented people (Acts 6:1–6). The twelve apostles quickly realized the church required more than talking about Jesus. This new group of varying personalities, nationalities, and beliefs would have a lot to learn, yet they knew the primary need was teaching and prayer (Acts 6:2).

Today, we are far beyond needing to form a church from scratch, yet we must remember no church can be perfect. Throughout the history of the church, the body of Christ has faced unknowns (such as denominational differences, cultural differences, political opinions, and false teachers, to name a few) requiring God's guidance and wisdom. To expect any church to wisely handle every need or to perfectly know God's will without question is unrealistic. As a result, we need God's courage to risk being involved in a group of people who will disappoint us, and who we will disappoint.

The conflict of Acts 6:1–6 is an example. The Hellenists, Greek-speaking Jews, believed their widows were being "neglected in the daily distribution" (Acts 6:1). Some commentators believe the reference to serve "tables" (*trapezais*) (6:2) can refer to food and/or money. In Matthew 21:12 and John 2:15, where Jesus overturned the money "tables," the same Greek word is used. Therefore, the issue might refer to the actual serving of food and someone sitting at a "table" distributing money and provisions for widows and others in need.

The incident could also point to a certain level of prejudice against those who didn't speak Aramaic, the common language of most Jews. We might safely assume some of the widows couldn't adequately express their needs. Or they were fearful because of their past traumas, because widows were the most vulnerable group in society. Even today, we may not perceive the needs of others because they don't express themselves for fear of rejection.

When the apostles became aware of the difficulty, they quickly responded by forming a committee, including Stephen, that took responsibility over the problem.

6. What challenges did Stephen face (Acts 6:8–15)?

A. Describe the kind of courage Stephen needed to stay true to God.

B. Stephen faced the most drastic kind of persecution. What other kinds of persecution do Christians suffer even today?

C. Have you ever experienced what you believed was persecution for your faith in God, even if it didn't result in physical harm?

D. How did you gain courage to go through your trial?

When we suffer for Christ's sake, we might think we should dismiss the pain of our suffering by comparing our situation to others who have suffered more. We can always find those who suffer more or less than us. But focusing on the level isn't helpful for growing in dependence upon God. He invites us to acknowledge the opposition or obstacle to remind us to call upon him. Then our trust in him can grow.

7. What are some of the reasons Christians meet together?

   A. I Corinthians 16:1–3:

   B. Hebrews 5:12:

   C. Hebrews 10:24–25:

   D. Hebrews 13:7:

   E. Hebrews 13:17:

   F. James 5:13–15:

   G. James 5:16:

H. James 5:19:

8. Do you disagree with any of those reasons?

9. Which one is most meaningful to you?

10. How do the following verses from Galatians 6 guide us in how to encourage others in the body of Christ?

    A. 1:

    B. 2, 5:

    C. 6:

    D. 9:

E. 10:

F. Are you disobeying any of those commands? If so, what will you do about it?

G. How does courage factor into obeying these commands?

Galatians 6:1 is both a command and a warning. God commands us to help someone leave a sinful pattern. We must guard against feeling smug that we aren't sinning like someone else. Because every sin is rebellion against God, we cannot regard our own "small" sins to be less important than the sinful choices of others. We are all equal as we kneel before the cross of Christ. If we think we are immune, we are weaker than if we acknowledge we can be tempted. A blind eye to our own temptations opens us to be caught in sin's subtle traps.

The Bible addresses hard issues and doesn't ignore problems. God isn't shocked about the problems we face. Although different sins create different degrees of consequences, God identifies any and every disobedience with the same word: sin.

Our loving Heavenly Father doesn't have unrealistic expectations of his people. He provides direction for problems, including those within the church. He doesn't want us to ignore the sinful patterns church members face.

God wants us to take appropriate action to help others. To acknowledge we could sin like anyone else takes courage because so often we want to be seen in a good light.

The truths of Galatians 6:2, 5 can initially appear contradictory. On the one hand we are told to bear one another's burdens, but then also that each person should bear their own load. A helpful distinction can be defining a "burden" as a challenge someone isn't strong enough yet to handle. They haven't progressed in their spiritual life enough to persevere without help.

A "load" on the other hand, can be thought of as something a person is mature enough to defeat on their own. Doing so will increase their dependence on God and decrease their inappropriate dependence on people. These distinctions take a great deal of wisdom to identify.

11. Read the following verses.

    A. Psalm 49:7

    B. Proverbs 19:19

    C. Proverbs 22:24–25

    D. Proverbs 26:17

The previous four selections of verses give a broader perspective for responding to struggling believers than we might usually consider. Often, we think we must respond to every need a Christian has and make sure she does the right thing, even to the point of feeling responsible for her choices. The wisdom from these verses can give us courage to do what might seem uncomfortable yet might be best for her.

For instance, Psalm 49:7 assures us we can't be another person's redeemer or give a ransom for them. Only Jesus qualifies because only he was sinless and could die for our sins, plus have the ability to sanctify us. Our courage can increase as we realize God can fulfill within another person what we can't.

Proverbs 19:19 emphasizes how protecting an angry person from the consequences of her choices could encourage her to continue sinning. God will give us the courage to allow her to "pay the penalty," knowing only then she'll see the error of her ways.

Proverbs 22:24–25 warns us there are limits to the level of friendship that is best with certain people. We can be acquaintances, but we must put up a guard against being a close friend who has the possibility of influencing us. Knowing this guideline will give us courage when God says to limit contact.

Finally, Proverbs 26:17 strengthens our courage to choose associations wisely by knowing not every battle of others is ours to fight. People may try to convince us their "dog" is ours to protect, but only God knows his assignments for us.

From these verses, we can have confidence knowing other people don't need to dictate our choices. God will guide us.

12. How do the previous verses personally give you courage and wisdom for any current situation?

13. Read I Corinthians 12.

   A. What is the purpose of the gifts of the Holy Spirit (v. 7)?

   B. Verses 12–27 stress the metaphor of the church as a body. What problem can occur if we judge one gift or role as superior over the others (vv. 15–19, 24–25)?

C. Why should we be content with the gift or role God has given us within the body (v. 18)?

D. Why is every member of the body of Christ needed (vv. 15–20)?

E. What do Christians sometimes think which diminishes courage (vv. 21–23)?

F. What is God's desire for every member of the Body (vv. 25)?

G. What is a solution for the problem expressed in verses 21–24?

H. How have you seen verse 26 be true in your church or study group?

Because of this essential chapter in I Corinthians, we can be resolute in knowing God wisely chooses giftings for each believer. We can confidently resist comparing our gift to another gift or being envious of another's calling.

Every single person has value because we all are image bearers of God. Being an "image bearer" means we are made in God's image, the foundation for our true worth, not our giftings. God will provide and equip us for our calling to fulfill his plan and give himself glory.

14. Based on I Corinthians 12, what is your gift?

A. How have you struggled with using your gift?

B. How have you had courage to use your gift?

C. How did you discover you have that gift?

Here are some truths to support your courage about your spiritual gifting. First, God never assigns spiritual gifts based on our worthiness or human skill. His goal is to provide for the needs of his Body so that the church can operate in holiness to magnify God, not make someone look good.

Second, fight against fear of making a mistake. No one uses their spiritual gift perfectly. Even if we view someone as effective, it doesn't mean they perfectly follow God's leading. We all err in some way. Don't compare yourself to others.

Third, we shouldn't conclude we've chosen the right gift based on results. Sometimes God allows obvious results. But a lack of "fruit" doesn't mean we are misusing our gift, or we identified the wrong one. Judging our effectiveness by what happens isn't a wise perspective.

Fourth, we must resist taking the opinions of others as the only guidance indicating our spiritual gift. Although we should consult with those who have wisdom, we can ask and trust God will direct us also. If we attempt to use a gift, and yet, it doesn't seem to connect with us initially, we don't need to be discouraged. God may want us to learn over time how to use a gift. If after time we still are confused or God isn't opening doors, we might need to reconsider.

God's plan for ministry must have shocked the emerging church. Most likely some people had difficulty accepting the "inferior" people of society as equals. But how like God's plan to value everyone and go against the harmful rules of society. New Christians needed a lot of courage to set aside the influence of culture and use God's spiritual gift.

For deeper study: Study these passages for listings of spiritual gifts: Romans 12:6–8; I Corinthians 12:8–10; I Corinthians 12:28–30; Ephesians 4:11; I Peter 4:10–11.

15. From the following passages, record some of the relational struggles the early church experienced.

   A. Acts 15:36–41; 2 Timothy 4:10–11:

   B. Galatians 2:11–14:

   C. Philippians 4:2–3:

   D. Philippians 4:15:

   E. II Thessalonians 3:10–12:

16. What surprises you about the conflicts these strong Christians experienced?

17. How does knowing about these conflicts strengthen or hinder your courage to persevere in attending church and facing possible relationship problems?

The conflict between Paul and Barnabas can be disconcerting (Acts 15:36–41). They had already been ministering side by side and traveling together for years. Paul's love of churches influenced him to conclude Mark's abandonment put the ministry at risk. Of course, he loved individuals, but Barnabas's love for the individual was greater. The fact Mark was Barnabas's relative also must have contributed to Barnabas's loyalty to Mark.

Barnabas's name means "son of encouragement," and he was known for encouraging everyone around him. He knew John Mark was overwhelmed by the demands of ministry and didn't have the spiritual maturity to be steadfast. Barnabas's people-loving nature wanted to build up the faint-hearted.

Both Paul and Barnabas were right ... and wrong. They loved all aspects of ministry but in this situation, their commitment valued one aspect as more important than another. Paul saw the big picture of the church's needs. Barnabas saw the little picture of the individual within the church. Knowing their bents, we can understand how each contributed an important part for a wholesome, effective ministry.

God wasn't caught short when the two leaders separated. Paul took Silas with him, and Barnabas took Mark. The outreach was doubled. Later, Mark became associated with Peter, and Mark ended up writing the Gospel account entitled "Mark," based on the information Peter gave him. Plus, Paul learned to value Mark so much that later he wrote of Mark's "helpfulness" (2 Timothy 4:11).

Notice in 2 Timothy 4:10, Paul comments Demas "deserted" him. The Greek word is "forsaken," meaning to "utterly abandon with the sense of leaving someone in a desperate situation." Yet Paul persevered.

If anyone had reason to say, "Why should I go to church, everyone there is imperfect," it was Paul. Only keeping his eyes on Jesus kept Paul faithfully serving imperfect people. Paul knew he wasn't serving people; he was serving God who would never desert him. Such confidence can empower us to persevere in serving an imperfect group of people making up the church.

18. Read John 18:15–18, 25–27; 21:15–17.

   A. After Peter denied his association with Jesus, what do you think Peter expected Jesus's response to be toward him?

   B. Why do you think Jesus had the courage to use Peter even though Peter had proven himself unreliable and fearful?

   C. In what ways does Jesus's example of delegating his mission to imperfect people like Peter give you courage as you think of your responses to other imperfect Christians?

D. How does reminding yourself you also are imperfect and yet forgiven, like Peter, give you courage to know God wants to use you?

Having courage within the imperfect church requires trust in a perfect God. Even though there are many arguments and disagreements within the Christian church across the world, we can have courage to continue serving God to the best of our ability and understanding because we know God knows the plan. We serve a faithful, wise, and wonderful God.

My Precious Princess and Daughter:

You are a part of my body, the church. My beloved Son, Jesus, is the head, and you are an important and essential part of the church's influence upon this world. My family can't function as effectively without you because you bring to it the personally crafted skills and talents I gave to you. It may seem like such a big organism doesn't need you, but that's not true. Every child of mine is responsible to contribute to my body.

I knew from the beginning my body wouldn't function perfectly. Human sinfulness and selfishness are like a disease within it, and I know the church will never be perfect. Yet, my plan is effective because of my power. I am the source of its courage. I want you to be a part of my glory as you contribute according to my calling upon you and my plan.

Don't focus on the weaknesses of the church. Instead, focus on how I want to use you within it and outside of it to represent me to a confused, blinded world. You may feel like a small toenail, but I have important work for you to accomplish for me. Every part of the whole is equally important and useful.

Let my forgiveness of you give you the courage to forgive others. You aren't perfect and neither are your brothers or sisters in Christ. You need each other.

I love you, and I love all my children equally. Live with a courageous heart.

Lovingly,
Your Heavenly Father, the King

~Lesson 6~
Courageously Standing Against Popular Opinion

Most of us want to be popular and considered valuable. Because people might not like us, we fear going against the opinions of others. Today, maybe more than ever, expressing ideas that don't match up with current worldly beliefs can bring harsh consequences.

Even if the consequences aren't major, standing strong in what we believe can cause us to be rejected, excluded, and blocked on social media. With the internet, our reputation can be quickly smeared, while we are powerless to prevent the lies.

The biblical characters we will be studying in this lesson may not have had to contend with social media, but they still suffered because they obeyed God. Their strong courage is an inspiration for us. Let's see how we can diminish our people-pleasing to value God's opinions of us more than anything people offer us.

1. What ideas or attitudes generally respected by society go against the standards of God's Word?

A. Have you ever done something in obedience to God that went against popular opinion? What was it? What happened?

  B. Have you ever disobeyed God to go along with sinful popular opinion? What did you do and what happened?

2. Read Exodus 1:15–22.

  A. How did these two women disobey Pharaoh in obedience to God?

  B. Why were their actions a stand against popular opinion (1:12–13)?

  C. Do you think the midwives lied or do you think there's another explanation?

  D. Do you think there are times when lying is justified? If so, for what situations?

E. How and why would God reward their actions?

F. How do you think fearing God contributes to having courage to obey him?

As is common in many stories in the Bible, the written account doesn't declare whether a choice is wrong or right, only what occurred. We don't know if God directly commanded the midwives to disobey the Egyptian king. We only know they "feared God" (1:17) which empowered their lack of fear for human authority.

But how do we reconcile servants of God lying? After all, we know God never lies (Titus 1:2) and never honors deceitfulness. Yet, God did reward the two midwives who lied. But did they really lie? And did they "lie" at God's direction?

Maybe they didn't actually lie. Possibly they selectively said what was true—the Hebrew women gave birth before the midwives could arrive. Maybe the Hebrew women waited until the last minute to call the midwives as a means of protecting an infant.

Some commentators reason the two named midwives may have been the "senior" midwives of the total group of midwives. It's highly improbable only two midwives could serve the huge Hebrew population. Another possibility is that Shiphrah and Puah didn't murder the male babies, but others did. We don't know.

God doesn't give us all the details, so we don't have to figure everything out. Maybe this story is more about teaching us to fear God as the source of our courage. Scripture doesn't specifically say God rewarded them for lying, but for their fear of him (1:21).

How interesting the two courageous women who feared God are named, but the king of Egypt is unnamed in Scripture. Although Egyptian records indicate Thutmose I (1526–1512 BC) was most likely the Pharaoh at the time, God does not give him any honor by including his name.

Because Pharaoh's plan for killing the Hebrew male babies wasn't working, he told the Egyptian population to voluntarily throw Hebrew male babies into the Nile. Although this is horrifying to us, the command would not have been shocking to them. Infanticide was a common practice, because human life was not considered sacred. Whether any baby lived or died was decided by the father of the household. Female Egyptian babies were most often thrown out on the trash or into the river. The Israelites' value of life was in stark contrast to Egyptian culture.

Similarly, as God provided courage for the midwives, if any of us are called to do something against the dictates of society or government, God will give us the courage we need in the moment. We may not know exactly how we will respond, but he will direct us in the moment.

3. Read Exodus 2:1–10.

   A. Who were two other women who went against Pharaoh's law and what did they do? (One is a relative of Moses and one is not.)

   B. How did God reward Jochebed for her courage and creativity?

C. Why did Jochebed risk death by defying the Pharaoh's command?

D. What honor does Hebrews 11:23 give Moses's parents?

E. Do you think Pharaoh's daughter could have also suffered consequences? Why or why not?

F. Have you done or do you know of someone who has done something as bold? What was it?

Nothing would have culturally motivated the daughter of the Pharaoh (possibly Hatshepsut), to save the Hebrew child. After God gave her the initial curiosity and compassion for the crying baby, we can assume the Pharaoh's daughter had the power to go against her father's edicts. She may have convinced herself (and others) she wasn't going against her father's rule because she would raise Moses as an Egyptian not a Hebrew. But of course, every detail was designed by God to save the Israelites from their slavery decades later when Moses would lead them out of Egypt as a freed people.

We can wonder why the princess concluded quickly the baby was Hebrew. Several reasons tell us why.

- Circumstances: Only the Israelites would have needed to try to save a male child. Rarely was a male Egyptian child abandoned. Girl babies were the ones on the trash heap.
- Circumcision: The baby would be circumcised—a practice Egyptians weren't performing at that time.
- Characteristics: Differing physical appearance between the two groups.
- Compassion: God enlightened her understanding and sparked her empathy for this baby.

God's sovereign power is exalted even more as he uses only women to rescue Moses when women were not considered valuable in Egyptian culture. God may be telling us he offers his courage to all, male or female.

As the examples of these women show courage, our courage can grow from trusting God. If we face something dangerous to either our identity or even our life, we can be assured God is with us and orchestrating everything around us.

Even today there are martyrs. Christians around the world are being harmed and their lives disrupted because of their commitment to Christ. God is strengthening them now and will in the future for any of us who suffer in any form.

4. Read Joshua 2.

    A. What did Rahab do in opposition to the leaders of the city (vv. 1–6)?

    B. Why did she do that (v. 9)?

C. What was the foundation of her courage and faith (vv. 10–11)?

D. What motivated her choices (vv. 12–16)?

E. What happened to Rahab and her family (Joshua 6:22–25)?

F. Why would God include Rahab in his "hall of faith" in Hebrews 11:31? What does that say to you?

As we examine Rahab's lying, we can't use the same reasoning we did about the midwives possibly not lying. Rahab intentionally lied and misled the king's messengers to protect and save the two Israelite spies. Canaanite culture approved of lying; she most likely didn't think twice about it. Regardless of cultural standards (or lack of them), the commands of the Bible stand firm. We can never use cultural viewpoints as an excuse to diminish our commitment to God's holiness. God wants to strengthen our courage to stand for him regardless of any consequences we fear.

As we study this story, we could wonder why the king's messengers did not search all of Rahab's home, especially her bedroom. The customs of the day regarded a woman's bedroom as a private place no one could enter. Rahab was known as a harlot, and some commentators think the Hebrew word *zonah* for harlot can also indicate an innkeeper, which would go along with the fact the spies "lodged there" (v. 1). What better place for them to stay, because a lot of people would be going in and out. God used these aspects of the Canaanite culture for his own purposes and advantages.

Even though Rahab's lying was wrong, we must acknowledge her courage. She knew very little about the God of the Israelites, and yet what she knew was enough to prompt her to risk her own life. Nor did she know God well enough to trust she didn't have to lie—that he could provide some amazing plan to protect his people.

Our goal as Bible students should not be to vindicate her lying. She did sin. But her knowledge about God was limited. If she was indeed an innkeeper, she'd heard stories from travelers about the Israelites and their powerful God. The stories weren't the only influence to inspire her belief. The very Spirit of God was at work.

Her belief didn't mean she became completely victorious over every sin. We might try to reason, "Well, lying was the only option available to save the spies." Such an idea is like saying God couldn't think of any other solution. As a creative God, he could have fashioned any number of solutions.

The primary biblical message of Rahab's deeds is how God saves a sinner and gives her courage to protect his people even if imperfectly. God drew her to himself through the stories of his favor for his chosen people. He gave her faith, but it didn't mean she would never sin.

What a marvelous assurance for us because we come to Christ for salvation, and God knows the process of spiritual dependence upon him has only begun. The midwives were honored and blessed because they feared God. And Rahab is included in the "hall of faith" (Hebrews 11:35) because of her faith, not her perfect behavior. We are saved based upon our faith in Jesus as our Savior, not because we earned our way through perfect living.

After the Israelites protected Rahab and her family when they destroyed Jericho, Rahab married Salmon, who most commentators believe was one of the spies. This couple are a part of the lineage of Jesus. Matthew 1:5-6 tells us, "… and Salmon the father of Boaz by Rahab, and Boaz the father of Obed by Ruth, and Obed the father of Jesse, and Jesse the father of David the king." What a fascinating love story.

Rahab is an example of God's grace in using a forgiven sinful woman in the ancestral line of Jesus. May we never forget no one is beyond God's gracious touch or unable to receive his courage.

5. What purposes are accomplished when we reflect on and share with others what God has done for us?

   A   Psalm 40:1–4

   B. Psalm 40:10

   C. Psalm 77:11–14

D. II Corinthians 10:15–17

   E. II Corinthians 12:9–10

6. How do you ask God for his courage to tell others about your faith and God's work in your life?

7. How do you think your sharing could give courage to others?

8. Read Matthew 1:18–19 and Luke 1:26–38.

   A. Why did it take courage and obedience for Mary to accept the role God chose for her?

   B. How does Leviticus 20:10 explain the danger she was in?

dependence upon him has only begun. The midwives were honored and blessed because they feared God. And Rahab is included in the "hall of faith" (Hebrews 11:35) because of her faith, not her perfect behavior. We are saved based upon our faith in Jesus as our Savior, not because we earned our way through perfect living.

After the Israelites protected Rahab and her family when they destroyed Jericho, Rahab married Salmon, who most commentators believe was one of the spies. This couple are a part of the lineage of Jesus. Matthew 1:5-6 tells us, "... and Salmon the father of Boaz by Rahab, and Boaz the father of Obed by Ruth, and Obed the father of Jesse, and Jesse the father of David the king." What a fascinating love story.

Rahab is an example of God's grace in using a forgiven sinful woman in the ancestral line of Jesus. May we never forget no one is beyond God's gracious touch or unable to receive his courage.

5. What purposes are accomplished when we reflect on and share with others what God has done for us?

  A   Psalm 40:1–4

  B. Psalm 40:10

  C. Psalm 77:11–14

D. II Corinthians 10:15–17

   E. II Corinthians 12:9–10

6. How do you ask God for his courage to tell others about your faith and God's work in your life?

7. How do you think your sharing could give courage to others?

8. Read Matthew 1:18–19 and Luke 1:26–38.

   A. Why did it take courage and obedience for Mary to accept the role God chose for her?

   B. How does Leviticus 20:10 explain the danger she was in?

C. How does the angel's response (Luke 1:36–37) to Mary's question (Luke 1:34) help to give Mary courage?

D. How does Elizabeth's instant reply, and her baby's movement, give Mary further courage (Luke 1:41–45)?

Unless we understand the horrible consequences Mary anticipated if she became pregnant, we can't fully grasp the depth of her courage. Although it seems she quickly acquiesced to God's will, we mustn't forget she could have rejected his plan. She did express wonder at how such a plan could be fulfilled. She didn't doubt; she was only curious. She didn't question the assignment; she only wondered about the details.

The life-threatening danger Mary would face was not because she would be pregnant. Because she was betrothed to Joseph, it wasn't a death penalty if they were sexually active. Technically by Jewish law, being "betrothed" meant they were legally married even if they weren't yet living in the same house. Some researchers have found Jewish writings accepting the idea that a betrothed couple could be sexually intimate in the bride-to-be's home.

The problem was Joseph knew he wasn't the father of the baby, thus making Mary an adulteress—she must have been sexually intimate with another man. Thus, she could be stoned to death as the Levitical law determined. That's why Joseph planned to save her by divorcing her quietly to avoid making a shameful spectacle of her. To protect her, God sent his angel to tell Joseph in a dream Mary hadn't done anything wrong. They should go ahead and go through with the marriage ceremony. We don't know when that happened, but most likely before Mary left to visit Elizabeth.

9. Read Mary's song in Luke 1:46–55.

   A. What characteristics of God does she mention which were the foundation for her courageous trust in his plan for her?

   B. Which of your beliefs about God are the foundation for your courage and willingness to suffer public ridicule to fulfill his plan for your life?

   C. Have you ever been misunderstood or ridiculed for your faith? Explain.

When we examine the details of Luke 1, we see the many ways God encouraged Mary's obedience.

- 28, 30: calls her favored. He is assuring her that her pregnancy will not mean a death penalty.
- 1:28: God is with her; he has not abandoned her.
- 1:30: acknowledges her fear but doesn't shame her for it.

- 1:31–33: gently explains the reason for this calling, the glorious coming of his Messiah.
- 1:35: kindly responds with an explanation.
- 1:36: speaks of God's miracle that her barren relative Elizabeth who is past child-bearing years is pregnant. If he could give Elizabeth a miracle, then he could provide for Mary.

10. From Mary's song of praise, known as "The Magnificat," we see how she rehearses God's attributes to build her faith.

    - v. 47: savior
    - v. 48: sovereign control
    - v. 49: mighty and holy
    - v. 50: merciful
    - v. 51: strong
    - v. 52: just
    - v. 53: generous
    - v. 54: helpful and merciful
    - v. 55: communicator

To develop our courage, we can benefit from studying truths about who God is. If we are without courage, we may be believing lies about his qualities. By correcting those lies, we will have greater confidence to be bold for God and obey him.

11. What reasons do each of these verses give us for being courageous?

A. Deuteronomy 31:6

B. Joshua 1:7–9

C. II Chronicles 15:7

D. Psalm 27:1

E. John 14:1–3

F. John 16:33

G. Romans 8:31

H. Which of those is most meaningful to you?

11. Based on those facts, in what specific way will you respond with more courage in your present challenge?

12. Read John 2:13–17, 23–25.

    What godly principles are revealed from these verses about how Jesus courageously stayed strong against popular opinion?

13. From the biblical women studied in this lesson, which woman's courageous dependence on God is the most meaningful to you? Why?

Worldly opinions, cultural perspectives, and the ideas of those around us can influence us more than we think. Our bravery in standing strong for God's ideas is not easy. Living by faith and not by sight challenges us almost every day when we are bombarded by the ungodly messages from television, social media, and the opinions of others. We may not be in danger of our lives, but even feeling like our worth and value are being questioned can damper our desire to seek and obey God.

May the godly truths we have studied in this lesson deepen our belief God knows best. Knowing his unconditional love, protection, and wisdom will help us fight against the lies which threaten our faith in God's ways.

My Precious Princess and Daughter:

I understand your deep desire to be accepted and loved, yes, even popular and well-liked. I developed longing within you, so you would want to seek me for your acceptance. People may meet some of your needs, but only I can give you the total satisfaction and happiness you want. Ultimately, I'm the only one capable of meeting all your expectations.

Let my love give you courage when standing strong for me and my unchanging truths, even if you become less popular in this world dominated by sin.

I empowered those biblical women to obey me in a society that did not esteem them. They were courageous even when they might be misunderstood and persecuted. I want to give you courage—courage to live a godly life and courage to speak of me boldly, wisely, and fearlessly.

Your words and example are vehicles I use, but my Spirit creates the impact. You are my beloved daughter. Cling to our family values and obey me because you love me. I promise I will take care of you.

Lovingly,
Your Heavenly Father, the King

~Lesson 7~
Courageously Standing Against Evil

At times the world around us feels out of control and pointless because evil seems to be winning. We feel afraid and powerless, wondering if our small voices are being heard. Our courage withers. We wrestle with which, if any, issues we should fight for. And then, how do we make a stand? We know God is a righteous God and yet, governmental confusion makes us wonder if he really cares or is fighting against evil.

Let's see how God wants to highlight his own just and righteous nature as revealed in his Word. We know the Bible applies to every area of our lives. In his Word, we uncover his guidance to know how God wants us to courageously stand against evil.

1. What irreverent and unprincipled ideas do you see being valued in the world?

    A. What feelings do you experience seeing the state of the world?

B. What blocks you from following God's direction regarding addressing evil in the world?

C. What would it take for you to stand against forces of evil as God directs?

2. Scan the book of Esther. What evils and danger did Esther and the Jews face (3:8-9, 13)?

A. What did Mordecai want Esther to do (4:8)?

B. Why is Mordecai's command dangerous (4:11)?

C. Does the phrase, "for such a time as this" in 4:14 strengthen your courage in any way?

D. What did Esther finally decide, and what qualities of courage did she exemplify (4:16)?

E. How did Esther reveal a dependence upon God even though his name is not mentioned (4:16)?

F. How did God protect Esther (5:2)?

G. What courageous plan did Esther put into effect (5:4, 7–8; 7:3–6; 8:3–6)?

H. Why do you think Esther carries out her plan in stages?

I. How is God working behind the scenes (2:5–7, 5:9–6:10)?

J. How are the Jews saved (8:10–17, 9:5)?

K. How did Esther influence her people by her actions (chapters 9–10)?

L. Have you felt like God has ever used you for a special plan and purpose? If so, explain.

M. As you think of the current world or past world history, are there any similarities with Esther's story (in broad generalities?)

At the beginning of Esther's story, she had no idea she and her people would face life-threatening danger. She walked step by step in faith. Esther's journey is the same for us. We don't know the future, or how God wants to use us. We can only faithfully follow through on the guidance we receive. Knowing God's orchestration behind the scenes in Esther's story can build our courage.

Today, we may not be able to see God's work, but stories like Esther remind us God is always at work. He never feels worried or confused. He is totally in control. That's the basic definition of his sovereignty: he is totally in control.

Here are some of the examples of God's sovereignty.

- Rejection of Vashti as queen thus setting up the search for a new queen (chapter 1).
- Favor of king toward Esther out of the many women he could choose from (chapter 2).
- Haman hated the Jews (chapter 3). It may seem strange God would allow someone to plan evil, but in the end the plan is defeated thus giving God glory.
- The king can't sleep and requests some of the chronicles of his reign be read (chapter 6). At this point, he's been in power for twelve years. The reading about Mordecai was five years earlier, yet that story is the one chosen by God's design.
- Mordecai wasn't given any reward when he saved the king's life (chapter 2). God would later use the "mistake" to give Mordecai favor with the king (chapter 6).
- When the king wants to honor Mordecai, Haman enters the outer court precisely then (chapter 6), and he must honor Mordecai.
- The king enters the room at exactly the time when it appears Haman is attacking Queen Esther (chapter 7), thus causing the King's anger and Haman's demise.
- The hearts of the enemies of the Jews are changed to favor them (chapter 8).

We don't know to what degree Esther had insight to understand God's orchestration, but certainly much of what happened must have given her courage to proceed with God's leading.

So often we don't think we have courage because we aren't taking huge steps. But Esther's story can speak to us how God leads one step at a time. He brings the results he wants in his timing.

One step she took seems unusual—have the king and Haman come to dinner two times. Commentators offer several possible reasons.

- She was led specifically by God.
- She was intimidated at the first dinner and didn't have the courage to follow through on her plan.
- She believed the pleasures of two delightful and delicious banquets would prepare the king's heart to hear her request and be more favorable toward it.
- The ploy emphasized the importance of her request.
- The delay piqued the King's curiosity and interest.

Of course, we don't know the reason(s) because Scripture doesn't spell them out. Ultimately, the "why" or "how" isn't important. The essential vital message is God will fulfill his plan to save the Jews.

Our courage will grow if we are convinced God will fulfill his plan. Ultimately, we really don't have the power to prevent or aid God's will. If we did have that level of power, we would be his substitute, a god. No one and nothing can substitute for the Lord God Almighty.

We can also have greater courage knowing even if we make a mistake or don't follow through with the right plan (like Esther possibly did), God can overcome any obstacle or mistake on our part. He knew from the beginning how he would save his people, to whom he had promised his loyal protection in the first covenants with Noah (Genesis 6:18) and Abraham (Genesis 15).

3. How do the following women each represent a category of evil choices or power over others?

Verses	Woman	Choice or Influence
Genesis 39:6–18		
Judges 16:4–18		
I Kings 19:1–3; 21:5–14		
II Chronicles 22:1–3, 10		
Mark 6:14–29		
Acts 4:36–5:11		

A. Pick one of the women and describe how her generalized wrong kind of a choice is carried out in our world today.

B. Have you experienced being spiritually attacked in the same way one of those women attacked another or made a sinful choice?

So far, we've seen how the Bible honestly points to those who had courage to do the right thing and those who didn't. God is showing us the destruction from wrong choices and the blessings of courageous wise choices. His Word also provides practical assurances for why we can trust him to provide courage.

4. What truth(s) from the following verses give you courage and how? Notice the possibilities of who God says he is, what our choices could be, and what the results might be from depending upon him.

   A. Deuteronomy 31:6

   B. Psalm 46:1, 10–11

   C. Isaiah 35:3–4

   D. Isaiah 41:10, 13

   E. Daniel 11:32b

   F. Colossians 4:2–3

   G. Hebrews 13:6, 8

When we consider Psalm 46:10, we often think of "be still" as an encouragement to slow down and spend time with God. That can certainly apply.

But the Hebrew word for "still" is *rapa* and refers to "to sink, relax, hang limp, let go, abandon, wait in weakness." There's the sense of surrendering our own plans and perspective. We are challenged to view ourselves in the light of knowing we are inadequate in ourselves in comparison to God's power, who will be exalted as he deserves.

Some translations use phrases like "cease striving" (NASB), "stop your fighting" (CSB, HCSB, GNT), "calm down" (CSV). Often our courage is diminished and destroyed by restless thinking as we try to enforce our own plan. The phrase indicates a command to "Stop!" and "that's enough." The Holy Spirit urges us, "You're forgetting God is God. Nothing will stop us being exalted; nothing will stop our plan. Have courage. Seek our guidance and everything will happen according to what we design."

Of course, we need to plan, but not when we are trusting in our own ideas. Sometimes we can know we are correctly following God's plan because we are at peace and have confidence in God's sovereign power. But our feelings are an inexact measure of whether we know God's will accurately.

Knowing we are in the confines of God's best plan gives us confidence to obey whatever he says and follow through, even when the challenge seems overwhelming. Notice the already established fact that God *will be* exalted. Courage comes from knowing nothing can stop God's plan. We are along for the ride as we obey.

5. Standing against evil may include courageously confronting a Christian brother or sister about sin in their lives.

A. What is necessary within our own hearts before taking any action (Matthew 7:1–5)?

B. What attitudes should we have that reflect God's attitude and motive (Matthew 18:10–14)?

C. What actions should we take when someone is sinning and unrepentant (Matthew 18:15–19)?

D. What will empower us to have the right motive as we confront (Matthew 18:21–35)?

E. What does the Apostle Paul advise about confronting a sinning person (I Corinthians 5:1–3)?

F. What warnings do you find important in Galatians 6:1–2?

If we know our hearts are purely motivated by wanting the best for another person, we will have courageous confidence to confront someone as God leads. If we are motivated for our own self-advancement or self-protection, then our judgment of others is sinful and not in alignment with God's will.

Matthew 7:1–5 in the Amplified Bible clarifies the intent (italic in the original):

> Do not judge *and* criticize *and* condemn [others unfairly with an attitude of self-righteous superiority as though assuming the office of a judge], so that you will not be judged [unfairly]. For just as you [hypocritically] judge others [when you are sinful and unrepentant], so will you be judged; and in accordance with your standard of measure [used to pass out judgment], judgment will be measured to you. Why do you look at the [insignificant] speck that is in your brother's eye, but do not notice *and* acknowledge the [egregious] log that is in your own eye? Or how can you say to your brother, 'Let me get the speck out of your eye,' when there is a log in your own eye? You hypocrite (play-actor, pretender), first get the log out of your own eye, and then you will see clearly to take the speck out of your brother's eye.

God is *not* saying, "Don't judge." In effect he is saying when you judge, judge righteously from a pure heart knowing you are susceptible to the very same thing and possibly even guilty yourself. Every single one of us kneels guilty before the cross and dependent upon Jesus's substitutionary death on our behalf. We will be able to wisely confront another if we first recognize sin in our own lives. Even if we aren't guilty of the same sin as another person, we have most likely sinned in that category.

In our present culture, judging others is misunderstood and misused. If Christians express an opinion against behavior God declares wrong, people say things like,

"You're not supposed to judge." "God is a tolerant, loving God." The objections are many. But many Bible verses talk about our duty to confront sin because our righteous God desires greater righteousness for the good of his creation.

To judge righteously, you should remind yourself:

- I don't know the heart—the motive—of the person whose behavior is sinful.
- What I judge might be the very thing that will tempt me.
- I should pray fervently before calling out the sin of others.
- I will ask questions rather than telling, accusing, or assuming.
- I won't wholeheartedly believe what other people say about someone. If God directs, I will talk directly to the person who is supposedly sinning.

6. From the following verses in Romans 8, identify truths which can give you direction when evil flourishes.

   A. v. 18

   B. vv. 19–22

   C. vv. 23–25

D. vv. 26–27

E. vv. 28–30

F. vv. 31–34

G. vv. 35–39

7. Which concept helps you the most?

8. How can you be strengthened specifically in the next week?

9. The Apostle Peter writes to Jewish believers who are being persecuted for their courage against evil. What wisdom does he want them to remember to give them hope and strength?

A. I Peter 4:12–16

B. I Peter 5:6–7

C. I Peter 5:8–9

D. I Peter 5:10–11

The Apostle Peter is writing to believers who live in Asia Minor. Asia Minor of Peter's day is the area of Turkey today. Tradition says Peter watched the crucifixion of his wife and purportedly said to her, "Remember the Lord." Peter wrote about suffering based upon his own experience. When Peter wrote his letters (epistles), he didn't know he would end up not only being persecuted but crucified. Tradition says that at his request, Peter was crucified upside down because he didn't consider himself worthy to be crucified in the same manner as Jesus.

In 64 AD, Nero would begin a horrendous persecution of Christians. Obviously, God's words through Peter were preparing them to be faithful and courageous as they would soon suffer in ways they couldn't anticipate.

Nero was the Roman Caesar for only fourteen years, but the damage his reign brought was disastrous. He was extremely evil and responsible for the deaths of many, including his mother, chief advisers, senators, and people in the noble class.

Historians aren't sure who started a fire that destroyed much of Rome. To turn away blame from himself, Nero accused Christians. Christians were killed by wild animals in large arena spectacles. At night on Roman streets, they were set afire on crosses to provide lighting. Nero was also known as morally bankrupt, giving into the worst kinds of immorality. He took his own life in AD 68 before the Senate could carry out its decree for his death.

10. Read Matthew 23:1–12; 37–39.

    A. What energized the evil of the Pharisees?

    B. What energized the goodness of Jesus?

11. Read Matthew 23:25–36.

    A. How and why do you think Jesus was empowered to courageously confront the Pharisees?

    B. When you are discouraged from standing strong for God's righteous ways, what is blocking you?

C. When you have stood strong for God's righteous ways, what strengthened you?

12. What truth(s) from this lesson will you apply?

13. In what specific situation do you think God wants you to stand against evil? How will you do that?

For many, the worldview of our culture brings the most intimidating situations a person faces. We think the world can't get any worse, and then, it does. We think Jesus must be coming immediately, but the days still pass by. Even when we see escalating evil, we can take courage to trust God is still in control. He will empower us to represent him with truth and righteousness at the right times.

My Precious Princess and Daughter:

You can make a difference in your world for me. I know evil and wickedness press in on you from every side, at times stealing your courage. They are not new threats. Only recycled and repackaged efforts by my enemy, Satan, to destroy your world and block you from representing me effectively.

But as my Son, Jesus, conquered Satan at Calvary, you, my empowered one, can also conquer the evil one's schemes and desires. You are victorious in my power, and nothing can stand against you. Satan might appear to be succeeding but take courage, for I am fighting the battle with you and already know the end of the story. The world's evil will not progress beyond my predetermined boundaries.

Do not be afraid. In quietness and confidence hold your ground. Although the devil may roar like a lion, he is an exposed roach on the floor of my antechamber. His influence is limited. In time, his evil will be fully destroyed, and my people will enjoy the perfect, sinless world of heaven.

Look expectantly for that day and continue to act by faith as a courageous senior officer in my army. I've won the battle. Victory is ours. Stand strong and act against evil.

Lovingly,
Your Heavenly Father, the King

~Lesson 8~
Courageously Standing for God at Work

For many women, working outside the home (and always in!) is not an option, it's essential financially. For the single woman or parent, work is a must for survival. For this lesson, let's also include a broader definition for "work." Volunteering, ministry, even hobbies could be included. Anything involving interaction with others is an opportunity for calling upon God's courage to represent him and choose godly reactions for his glory.

Any time we are a part of the lives of others, we can experience stressful challenges, which diminish our dependence upon God. Only he can help us with perfect wisdom and direction. From this lesson, let's use the questions, Scripture, and commentary to grow closer to God and trust him more. He wants to give us courage in everything we encounter in life, and maybe that's especially true for the distress of work.

1. Whether you're "working" by volunteering, church ministry, having a job outside the home, inside the home, or doing all ...

A. What do you like the most about one of these areas?

B. What do you like the least?

C. What is your greatest challenge in one of those areas?

2. Read I Kings 10:1–13.

   A. Why do you think God is including this story in his Word?

   B. What impresses you about the Queen of Sheba?

   C. What kind of courage do you think it took for this queen to seek wisdom from Solomon?

D. What qualities and attitudes as a ruler are revealed in her trip?

E. When you think of some unwise employers/managers, what contrasting qualities or attitudes to the Queen of Sheba do they have?

F. What resources for wisdom do you have as a Christian which strengthens your courage (James 1:5)?

G. If you are an employer or a person with any responsibility over others, what quality do you need to improve in your life, possibly inspired by Solomon or the queen? And to what degree does growing in godliness require courage?

There are some disagreements among historians and theologians about the location of the land/country of Sheba. Another area with a similar spelling, Seba, has been offered as the actual kingdom of the queen. In fact, Psalm 72:10 mentions both, "May the kings of Tarshish and of the coastlands render him tribute; may the kings of Sheba and Seba bring gifts!" But most experts believe Sheba was in Arabia, the western part of Asia, where Yemen is today. If so, the queen and her vast retinue traveled about 1,200 miles to reach Jerusalem.

But the location of Sheba isn't the most important aspect of this account. The essential element is the message God wants to communicate through this story. Remember, God is leading all the writers of the Bible to include certain stories and messages. There are endless other events available to be featured. God always has a specific purpose in each one.

For instance, this story in I Kings 10 is obviously about a woman. Wouldn't there have been many other male rulers who visited Solomon who were amazed at Solomon's wealth and wisdom? Yet God chose to focus on a woman. For any who call God a woman-hater, God is communicating his love for all. He created each person as his "image bearer," which gives every person intrinsic worth and value.

Even with the importance of that message, ultimately the primary purpose in everything in the Bible is to demonstrate who God is—his nature—and bring him glory. The phrase in verse 1, "concerning the name of the Lord," is the key. The story isn't merely about Solomon but how he reflected his God, Jehovah. In the ears and eyes of everyone who has heard of Solomon, the two are connected.

But how did so many hear about Solomon and his awesome God? As for the Queen of Sheba, news passed along through the trade routes reached her court. Sheba was in an area with a strong agricultural economy, and those traveling in and out doing business passed along the incredible news of Solomon and the God he depended upon. The Queen of Sheba had to know if the rumors were true. She had a hungry heart wanting to understand the truths of life. In fact, rulers at this time loved to talk philosophically about those very things. And evidently Solomon was known to be the best. Remember the story of the two prostitutes claiming one baby as their own (I Kings 3:16–28)?

These philosophical talks are referred to when the queen "told him all that was on her mind" (I Kings 10:2), and Solomon answered all her questions, completely satisfying and amazing her. This interaction is what verse 1 calls "hard questions," which can also be translated "riddles." She was longing to figure out the paradoxes of life, and Solomon knew the answers best. As a result, she spoke to Solomon acknowledging "the Lord your God who has delighted in you and set you on the throne of Israel" (I Kings 10:8).

The queen also acknowledged God's generosity who had provided Solomon's wealth, influence, and wisdom. God was being exalted as he should be. In her eyes, Solomon was the representative of his God.

As you and I work in whatever setting God has for us, we can call upon him for the courage to handle difficult people and situations boldly like Solomon did. We won't be perfect—even Solomon wasn't perfect—yet God graciously gave him everything he needed to bless God's chosen people, the Israelites.

First Kings 10 is a clear example of how the Bible contains layers of meaning. The story of the Queen of Sheba wasn't solely about her gaining wisdom but acknowledging what she longed for came from Solomon who was taught by Jehovah. The deepest reference is how the Bible points to the coming teacher, shepherd, and Savior, Jesus, who is completely wise and never sins nor makes mistakes.

As you study the Bible, look for layers of meaning. The ultimate deepest meaning is always about the Messiah Jesus. Jesus said in Matthew 12:42: "The queen of the South will rise up at the judgment with this generation and condemn it, for she came from the ends of the earth to hear the wisdom of Solomon, and behold, something greater than Solomon is here."

Jesus is pointing to himself as the ultimate reflection of God's nature because he himself is God, the Son of God.

The purpose of the book of Proverbs, which was written primarily by Solomon, is intended to teach and encourage wise and godly living by knowing the truth about God and how he intended life to be lived.

3. From the following verses in Proverbs, list information and/or benefits about wisdom and understanding.

   A. 2:9–11

   B. 2:12–15

   C. 3:13–15

   D. 3:16

   E. 3:17–18

F. 3:21–23

G. 3:24–26

4. Which of those verses is most meaningful to you? Why?

5. Which good quality do you want to grow stronger in? Which ungodly response do you want to diminish?

6. Which one gives you courage to be the godly person God wants you to be in an area of your life that is lacking strength?

7. Read Proverbs 31:10–31.

   A. What impresses you most about this influential working woman?

B. Do you think she does everything described at one time or over different seasons of her life? Explain the reasons for your answer.

C. Though she is a busy lady, do you think her family suffers? Why or why not?

D. What positive qualities does she have?

E. Which of her characteristics do you think gives her confidence to live courageously?

F. Which of her positive attitudes would you like to see strengthened in your life? How will you make that happen?

G. What kind of courageous choice is God asking of you currently in a stressful part of your life?

8. What theme do you notice in Proverbs 31:15, 18b, 27?

   A. How is this remarkable woman able to do all she does?

   B. How do you find a balance between diligent work and needed relaxation?

   C. No one always chooses wisely regarding the balance of work and rest. What do you think influences ungodly choices, and what do you think influences wise choices about work and rest?

   D. When you don't operate in that balance, what or who is influencing you?

Proverbs 31 describes a king's mother instructing her son on how to wisely choose a wife. She is giving a contrast between an ungodly wife (vv. 1–9) and a godly wife (vv. 10–31). She is basically telling him, "Don't be a fool to pick this kind of woman. Instead, be wise by picking this kind of woman." Most commentators believe King Lemuel is Solomon and his mother is Bathsheba.

Interestingly, she basically says, "Try to find the perfect godly woman but here's the bad news: she is impossible to find" (v. 10). We can easily conclude she's saying, "You won't find a woman who fits the bill perfectly but go for the woman who is closest to this description."

The description in verses 10–31 is of an apparently perfect woman who does it all—perfectly. We can become discouraged thinking we're supposed to completely measure up to this woman. But we must remember this passage describes her whole life over different seasons ... *and she has servants.* She is not doing all she does by herself. Yes, she is involved, absolutely. But she is also an administrator, delegator, and creator of projects. She sets the atmosphere and fragrance of the home, the palace, if she is indeed married to the king.

Therefore, before we judge ourselves harshly, let's remember this is a model we can move toward. God does not demand our perfection for us to have personal worth. God's final, most worthwhile description of her is her fear of him (verse 30). With that foundation, she will have courage and confidence to be both a worker and an administrator.

Traditionally in a Jewish home, these verses were recited by a husband and his children at the Sabbath dinner on Friday night every week. What a wonderful reminder and encouragement for the wife and mother of the home—and a training exercise for the girls of the family.

9. In the following verses of Proverbs, use "employer" for "the King" or "ruler" and note the principles a godly manager/leader should follow, regardless of your responsibilities.

   A. 20:8

B. 20:26

C. 20:28

D. 24:5

E. 24:6

F. 24:23–25

G. 28:16

H. 29:4

I. 29:11–12

10. In what ways do these principles strengthen your courage to obey God?

11. What weakness do you want to work on? Explain how it diminishes your courage.

12. Reread verse 20:8 and 26.

The concept of "winnowing" in 20:8 and 20:26 is a reference to the harvesting process of separating the wheat from the chaff. Proverbs 20:26 also refers to the threshing wheel, a part of the harvest activity. As the wheel rolls over the heads of grain, it helps to separate the chaff from the valuable wheat. The worthless chaff is then discarded. Likewise, the king separates the valuable, honest rulers from the wicked. He must wisely discern (spiritual "sight") (v. 8) to be able to identify the wicked and the good.

For all of us, whether we are working and serving in the home or outside, we need to ask God for wise discernment. We need wise courage to persevere getting rid of the "chaff" and using the "wheat."

13. What area(s) in your life do you need to winnow the wheat?

Work isn't always easy. There are difficult days and difficult people. We can become discouraged and less motivated to follow God's leading.

14. What principles and/or truths can you trust in from the following Proverbs verses? When applicable, note which responsibility each principle could apply to in your life.

   A. 15:3

   B. 16:3

   C. 21:1

   D. 21:2

   E. 22:29

   F. 25:15

   G. 29:25

H. 29:26–27

Courageous strength to fight against giving up, becoming discontent, or giving into ungodly impulses comes from knowing God is a God of power. He sees everything that is going on and cares. Even when we can't see him work, we can have courage to follow through with godly responses because we know he is our defender and always fulfills his will for our good and his glory.

15. What positive practices for your place of "work" can you find from these Proverbs verses?

   A. 11:3

   B. 12:19–20

   C. 15:1–2, 4

   D. 15:19

   E. 16:19

F. 18:13

G. 19:20

H. 20:19

I. 21:5

J. 24:17–18

16. Everyone would prefer to find great success and prosperity through their work, but what should be our motive (I Corinthians 10:31)?

17. Whether God blesses financially or not, what attitudes should you cultivate?

A. Ecclesiastes 5:18–20

B. Ecclesiastes 11:6

C. Philippians 4:11–13

D. Colossians 3:23–24

E. I Timothy 6:6–8

F. I Timothy 6:9–11

G. I Timothy 6:17

H. I Timothy 6:18–19

I. Hebrews 13:5–6

J. James 4:13–17

18. Pick one of those verse(s) and describe how courage is required to persevere in that/those attitude(s)?

19. How can you strengthen one of those attitudes in your life?

We can be tempted to have courage only if we receive results like riches, promotion, or approval. If our strength and joy are dependent upon those things, we will become easily discouraged.

Representing the Lord rightly often means faithful obedience even when we aren't acknowledged. We must trust God sees and is pleased with our courageous consistency.

Ultimately, we will be thrilled and satisfied with the rewards of heaven. The sweet victory of God's crown (Revelation 2:20, 3:11) will shatter any possible disappointment we think we might have. In those moments, we will only want the spotlight glowing on God's glory because he empowered everything good we did.

20. Read John 5:30–32.

   A. Why did Jesus have courage to "work" on earth?

   B. What was Jesus's motive to work?

   C. Whose approval did he seek?

21. As you think of the work you do (in whatever way God has called you) and the truths from this lesson, which one(s) is the most important to you in strengthening your courage to have a greater impact for Christ?

Jesus experienced in a general sense the feelings of every one of us, regardless of our responsibilities. He was the employee because he followed his Father's directions. He was an employer because he called together a band of workers who were imperfect.

We can never say Jesus doesn't understand the challenges we face. He experienced every kind of joy or obstacle a worker and boss faces. Let us be filled with courage to serve God in all the ways he assigns us. Our confidence and strength will be based upon serving our great God who knows everything and wants to support us for his glory.

My Precious Princess and Daughter:

I am so pleased with you. I see the desire of your heart to honor me, even if you don't think you do it perfectly. I will never give up on you, and my work in your life will continue until you join me in heaven. In the meantime, you're growing stronger and more able to obey me. Be encouraged. Whether you're serving me inside the home or outside or both, you represent me by your attitudes.

I know you don't always feel confident to represent me. But can you see the people problems and the stressful situations as opportunities to develop your trust in me? Every challenge is stretching you to diminish the need for the approval of others. Your work is ministry because I am leading you and using you to represent me everywhere you are.

You are my ambassador in whatever door I open for you. You are my representative in the home in which you live. Trust me. I know the plans I have for you. They will reap godly fruit within you and in those around you.

Never forget or ever doubt I love you and I am with you every day in every situation. You are my beloved daughter.

Lovingly,

Your Heavenly Father, the King

~Lesson 9~
Courageously Facing Temptation

Temptation. Something as obvious as a plate of chocolate chip cookies woos us. Other times, the smile from a man not our husband unnerves us. The possibilities for temptation are endless.

With so many enticements, the very thought of being tempted creates tension, even fear. At times, we knowingly give into temptation, and other times we are totally blindsided. We don't even realize we are being tempted. At yet other times, we are determined to resist and still our desires overwhelm us. Temptation can be simple or complex. Sometimes we wonder if we'll ever learn. Jesus resisted, why can't we?

Facing temptation can make us look inside ourselves and find the cornerstone upon which our lives need to rest. But we must have the right perspective about temptation. We need to understand temptation is not the same as sin—unless we give in to it. God is ready to help us with godly courage to resist temptation which hampers our influence in our world.

1. What are the most significant temptations you face?

A. When are you most likely to give in to temptation?

B. What do you feel is the most discouraging aspect of being tempted?

C. Does being tempted make you feel unworthy of influencing other's lives? Explain your answer.

D. How do you define temptation and how do you define sin?

E. What is the difference between temptation and sin?

2. What do these verses identify as opportunities for temptation?

A. Proverbs 6:16–19

B. Galatians 6:1

C. I Timothy 6:8–10

D. James 1:14–15

E. James 3:6

F. James 4:1–2

3. Read Genesis 3:1–6.

   A. Satan questioned God's command by saying (3:1):

   B. Satan changed God's message by stating (3:4):

C. Satan challenged God's goodness and wisdom by declaring (3:5):

D. How do you think each of Satan's ideas ate away at Eve's courage to trust God?

E. What kind of courageous thinking would have helped Eve and then Adam to resist the temptation?

F. How would you summarize Satan's strategies for tempting Eve?

Satan is always trying to attack God's character by questioning God's goodness, changing God's words, and challenging God's commands. Our enemy applauds when any of us wonders if God wants the best for us because he knows then we are vulnerable to disobeying God. Although doubt is not sin, it can lead to dwelling upon the times we wrongly concluded God acted contrary to who he says he is.

In those moments of believing lies about God, we are convinced we are safely protecting ourselves by disobeying him. Our courage falters and we lose our strength to believe God's promises, reflect upon his faithfulness in the past, and stand resolute.

4. Read Genesis 3:7–8.

   A. To what degree would you say a lack of courage contributed to the disintegration of happiness within Adam and Eve's marriage?

   B. What can you imagine the relationship between Adam and Eve was like right after they sinned?

   C. Can you personally make any connection between a lack of courage to obey God and a resulting struggle within your marriage and/or family?

Because Adam and Eve sinned, we—as a part of their lineage—have a sin nature, which desperately needs God's courage. With his help, we will be empowered to acknowledge our selfishness and learn more and more to trust him.

Thankfully God is not powerless to help. He wants to help us deal with what attracts and attacks us with his provision of truth. We are each wearing spiritual fig leaves trying to feel safe based on our own understanding. But total safety will never happen on this earth.

Only heaven, the "second" garden, will provide an absence of temptation. To expect lack of challenges now on earth will only blind our eyes to the dangers of temptation.

Trusting God requires courage to believe God is good. God called everything he had made "good" in the creation story. He also said it wasn't good for man to be alone. The word "good" is used numerous times in those first chapters of the Bible. God could have declared other positive words, but he chose "good" because his very being flows with goodness in his motives and actions. He can't do anything other than goodness because it is impossible for him to create something bad.

5. Read Genesis 3:8–24.

   A. When you are ashamed of your sin, how is your courage and influence on other's lives "covered up" and "hidden"?

   B. Even when you succumb to temptation, how does God respond to you as represented by his interaction with Eve and Adam (3:9)?

   C. What does his reaction and words show you about who God is, especially when you sin?

   D. What does he expect of you when you sin (3:10–11)?

6. Identify the three primary kinds of temptation in Genesis 3:6.

    A. In which category do you find yourself being tempted most often?

    B. Why is that category more enticing to you than the others?

7. Read Matthew 4:1–10.

    A. Who is being tempted?

    B. If this is new information for you, how do you feel and what are you thinking?

    C. If this is not new for you, is anything from those verses meaningful for you now?

D. In what three categories did Satan tempt Jesus and how did Jesus respond with each one?

a. vv. 3–4

b. vv. 5–7

c. vv. 8–11

8. Read I John 2:16.

A. What three categories of temptation are talked about in this verse?

B. Summarize what you've learned about the similarities of the three categories of temptation from the three passages.

I John 2:16	Genesis 3:6	Matthew 4:1–10
Lust of the Flesh		
Lust of the Eyes		
Pride of Life		

C. What surprises you about the similarities?

D. What do you find meaningful and applicable in these similarities?

When we identify the different categories of basic temptation strategies, we become strengthened knowing there's not much unknown to surprise us. We can have confidence knowing God wants to enlighten our minds and hearts to see Satan's ploys. He also empowers us to recognize our own sinful desires.

Here's a summary based on the three categories in I John 2:16 and how they refer to the temptations of Eve and Jesus.

- Lust of the flesh (craving for sinful physical pleasure or satisfaction):
  - Eve: Satan saying fruit will satisfy
  - Jesus: Satan saying Jesus should take his position and misuse it to satisfy himself with bread, which would be going beyond what the Father wanted for him at that time.
- Lust of the eyes (acquisition of earthly things with ungodly motives like coveting and envy):
  - Eve: Satan suggesting God had withheld something good from her and he didn't want the best for her. The fruit was the only thing withheld from her yet she felt neglected.
  - Jesus: Satan tempting Jesus to make a dramatic display so people would worship him—as if Jesus needed the worship.

- Pride of life (boasting, pride, ungodly desire for accomplishments, ambition, and position):
  - Eve: Satan suggesting she could be on the same level as God.
  - Jesus: Satan offering his own kingdoms to Jesus if Jesus would worship Satan. Satan was offering positions God was going to give Jesus anyway in his own method and timing.

9. As you think of the three categories above, which one is your primary weak point?

   A. Give a specific example of how you struggle the most in one of these categories.

   B. When you are being tempted, what ideas about God and his nature seem right but are wrong?

   C. From Matthew 4:4, 6, 10, how did Jesus fight against Satan?

   D. From II Corinthians 10:3–5, how should we fight Satan or our own inner compulsions?

E. What is important from James 1:13?

F. How can Hebrews 2:18 and 4:15–16 give you courage?

10. Read I Corinthians 10:13.

    A. What is the breadth of temptation's influence (13a)?

    B. How does God show his faithfulness and sovereignty (13b)?

    C. What promise do we have (13c)?

    D. How does Philippians 4:13 give insight into I Corinthians 10:13?

E. How do these truths give you courage to look at your own temptations and resist them?

Some people look at 1 Corinthians 10:13 and then are disappointed when they succumb to temptation. They think, "I thought God promised he wouldn't allow temptation beyond what I can resist. Therefore, I should never sin. God let me be tempted beyond my ability." Don't forget God also says he'll provide a way of escape.

This way of thinking interprets the verse as a promise of never experiencing circumstances or people beyond our own abilities. When we add in the mix of Philippians 4:13, which says God's power must be our source, we won't limit the potential of temptation. We also won't blame God when we stumble.

God will often allow circumstances stretching us into depending upon him even more. Many verses in the Bible talk about God allowing stronger problems than we normally face as a means of taking us deeper into dependence upon him (James 1:2–4).

We also must remember we need to take the Bible into account as a totality. If we only focus on one verse without regard for other verses, we could be led astray and then disappointed our expectations aren't met.

11. When we are tempted, what options do these verses offer us? How can each of these options help you resist temptation?

	Option	**Help Provided**
Psalm 119:11		
Matthew 6:13		
Matthew 26:41		
Romans 6:11–14		
II Peter 1:3–4		

12. If we do give into temptation and commit sin, of what can we be assured (I John 1:9)?

    A. Do you think there are "big" sins and "little" sins?

    B. Do you think God doesn't care as much about the "little" ones?

    C. Explain your answer.

13. Why does God want to forgive us?

    A. Isaiah 43:18–19

B. Isaiah 43:25

When we sin, we may feel discouraged and disappointed. But God doesn't.

When we have made some progress in the Christian life, we may think we won't succumb to the old lies and temptations. But every Christian is in a process of growth. There will be times of success when we feel confident. But there will also be times of falling back into areas of sin we thought we had overcome forever.

God is never caught unaware of our actions. He knew every moment of our lives before we were born, including our failings and successes. He can't be disappointed in us because disappointment includes having expectations. God knows we will struggle and even sin; exactly why he created the Gospel plan of salvation before he created the universe. Only heaven will be sinless. Here on earth, God patiently works with us in our journey. He put every sin—past, present and future—on the cross.

14. Although we cannot immediately forget our forgiven sin, what does God do (Psalm 103:3, 12; Isaiah 43:25)?

    A. Why do you think if we have repented of our sin, turned away from our sin, and God has forgotten our sin, we can't forget it?

    B. In contrast, what does our enemy, Satan, do (Revelation 12:10)?

C. Why do you think we agree with Satan's accusations?

D. What kind of wording does Satan use to specifically accuse you?

E. Based on Romans 8:1, 31–34, what does God say about you that is the opposite of Satan's messages about you?

F. What truths about God help you to take hold of God's courage when Satan accuses you?

Of course, God is aware of everything since he is omniscient and knows everything. Based on God "removing" our sin, he doesn't rehearse our sin. As humans, we cannot wipe memories of our sin away. Satan knows how to use the memory and the pain to remind and accuse us. His accusations are intended to discourage us, making us think God has given up on us. He also whispers we can't be forgiven if we do the same thing repeatedly.

Whenever we rehearse a previously forgiven sin, we can be assured God is not the one reminding us. He wants us to experience freedom from guilt because every sin was put on Jesus's cross and taken care of. Thankfully, the pain of our sin will diminish in time.

Don't let Satan continue to be your accuser. God is not believing him. You don't have to either.

15. Jesus's atoning death makes our forgiveness possible, but why does God forgive us according to these verses in Psalm 103? Make a note also of any characteristic about God's nature that is mentioned.

   A. v. 8

   B. v. 10

   C. v. 11

   D. v. 13

   E. v. 14

F. v. 17

16. What does Romans 3:23–25 indicate as the need of every person and the provision from God?

If you've never opened the door of your heart and asked Jesus to become your Lord and Savior, will you do so now? You can use this prayer as a model or pray to God with your own words.

> *Holy God, thank you for loving me so much that you sent your son, Jesus, to die in my place on the cross to pay the penalty for my sins. I recognize I am a sinner and need a Savior. Please forgive me of my sins. Cleanse me. Make me a new creature in Christ. I believe Jesus is your Son, died on the cross for my sin, was buried, and rose again from the grave to defeat the hold of sin and give me everlasting life. Thank you for coming into my life and becoming my Savior and the Lord of my life. In Jesus Name, I pray. Amen.*

17. If you prayed this prayer or put it in your own words, or received Christ as your Savior in the past, what has happened to you according to these verses?

    A. II Corinthians 5:17

B. Ephesians 1:3–4, 13

C. I Peter 1:18–21

D. I Peter 1:23

E. I John 5:11–13

F. I John 5:14–15

18. Based on this lesson, what will you do differently this next week regarding temptation?

Knowing we will be tempted for the rest of our earthly lives is both disheartening and comforting. It is disheartening because we know the journey of learning to resist is life-long and we won't arrive at perfection on this earth. But it is also comforting because we don't have to be shocked or surprised. We can anticipate and learn to identify the attacks of our enemy—and our own flesh. And we can also depend upon God's forgiveness which is always available.

My Precious Princess and Daughter:

I know the temptations you struggle with. I know the ones you give into far too easily, and the ones you wrestle to resist. Please remember you have power in my Son, Jesus's, name. Though you will always be tempted to some degree, you are learning to depend upon me more and more. Your courage is increasing.

Remember, I want only your good. Satan, our enemy, doesn't. He wants to destroy you and my creation. Ask me for wisdom so you may discern between trials coming to strengthen your faith and the temptations Satan sends intending to discourage you. He whispers enticing words. But his schemes end in pain.

He will try to tell you I'm keeping something good from you. But, my special daughter, will you believe I withhold nothing good from you? I could never plan anything for you that would harm or hurt you. That is against my character, therefore I won't harm you and I can't harm you. I am perfect goodness.

Yes, I will convict you of sin, discipline you, and train you to motivate and energize you to courageously trust and obey me. But I will never leave you nor forsake you. I never give up on you. Keep turning back to me.

Lovingly,
Your Heavenly Father, the King

Lesson 10
Courageous Jesus, Our Inspiration

Although we have referred to Jesus's courage in every lesson of this Bible study, there is still more we can learn from Jesus's example. We aren't surprised Jesus is the perfect example of courage, but we mustn't forget his humanity made it possible for him to sin. He could have lacked courage and disobeyed his Father. He had the capacity.

In fact, the possibility of him sinning is essential for God's salvation plan to work as he designed. Jesus must have the opportunity of choosing to trust his Father perfectly so he could take upon himself the sins of others on the cross. Otherwise, he could only die for his own sins, not the sins of others.

Because of Jesus's perfect responses, we can examine with assurance how God can help us. Let's look at different points of Jesus's life to see how he chose courage. As a human with desires like us, how could he be sinless? Scripture reveals the reasons, which can teach us. We won't choose perfectly, but we can grow in godly confidence.

1. Is it hard or easy for you to understand the significance of Jesus's potential for sin?

    A. How would you explain to someone the importance of Jesus being perfect as a human in order to be a substitute for the sins of the world?

    B. What does Hebrews 4:14–16 fit into this?

    C. How does knowing you can ask for help at God's throne through prayer give you courage?

As you study the events of Jesus's life in this lesson, try to picture yourself facing similar situations that he did. Jesus had available to him every bit of power he needed as God, but his humanity put him at risk as much as any of us. Every person has failed even as a Christian, but Jesus never failed because he resisted the lies of the world and his own human desires. Instead, he depended upon the truth of his Father's perspective.

Because of the Holy Spirit within us, we can call upon the same courage that strengthened Jesus.

2. We know the Christmas story of Jesus coming to earth as a human baby. Can you envision Jesus needing any courage to leave the perfections of heaven to enter the earth as a human?

   A. Does the fact Jesus knew everything about his life as a human affect your thoughts?

   B. If you knew your future, would you be more courageous or less?

3. Read Luke 2:41–52. Jesus is now twelve years old, at about the age boys begin to be considered men in Jewish culture. Jesus knows fully he is God incarnate and the purpose of his life. Yet his parents don't yet fully understand even though Jesus's miraculous conception and birth should have been enough information.

   A. Do you think Jesus risked anything by giving the response he did to his parents (Luke 2:48)?

   B. What kind of attitude or tone of voice do you "hear" in your head when you read Jesus's response to his parents?

C. How do you feel or think when you envision yourself at twelve giving the same kind of response to your parents? How would your motive and tone of voice mix into this?

D. When Jesus returned to his house with his parents, what truths and perspective might he have needed to be in submission to them (2:51)?

E. What is your opinion about what Jesus understood about his future?

Courage is only needed when there's risk. The danger can be physical, emotional, mental, and it can be real or imagined. Most often, the risk is because of how someone responds to us. Maybe we are misunderstood. Our motives are maligned, and we can't convince someone of our good intentions. We are treated as worthless. Our heart is wounded, and we feel powerless.

Now we're tempted to be discouraged and agree with the lies other people are saying about us. Our strength to keep telling ourselves the truth of God's unconditional love is depleted.

This kind of challenge could have occurred as early in Jesus's life as this situation with his parents. His parents were angry with him. They blamed him for their worry.

They lacked courage to trust God could keep his own Son protected. They must not have been fully convinced Jesus really was the Messiah. Otherwise, there wouldn't have been a need for worry. Where else would he be, as Jesus declared? Only one possible place, the temple.

Jesus, as a human, could have retorted in anger because of the lies his parents believed about him. In effect, they were saying, "You are foolish to have done this." "You put yourself in danger." "We can't trust you." Jesus's human side would want to defend himself. But his courage to resist defensive anger is based in knowing their lack of belief does not define him. We must "hear" Jesus's tone as being one of gentle sadness because their faith is weak.

The good news is Jesus's response was totally godly. With the human potential to sin, Jesus experienced as much need for courage as any human and could have been overwhelmed from the responses of others. He inspires us as we seek to resist the lies from others.

4. Read Luke 3:21–22. Can you think of several reasons Father God affirmed his Son?

    A. Can you think of a time when a sense of God's pleasure strengthened your resolve to obey him even though there was the possibility of some risk?

    B. When you face a God-given opportunity, how can this event give you courage?

5. Jesus has successfully resisted the three categories of temptations, which every human faces. (Luke 4:1–12). Satan was totally defeated and yet what does Luke 4:13 indicate will happen?

   A. Why do you think this information is important?

   B. Does this give you any insight or courage about the continuing temptations you face?

Although Jesus had successfully resisted his enemy's attacks in every category, Satan didn't give up. Although we don't have specific accounts of Satan tempting Jesus after this, the challenges Jesus faced requiring dependence upon his Father are temptations.

Don't be perplexed when you believe you are successful in some area and then stumble again in the same area. Sanctification, the process of spiritual growth, increases because we often face the same kind of temptation in different ways repeatedly. Such challenges don't mean we are abandoned. We can persist because we know God never gives up on us and never leaves us.

6. What does Jesus identify as his own calling (Luke 4:16–19)?

A. What does Jesus quickly address that is on everyone's mind (Luke 4:20–24)?

B. Have any longtime relatives or friends misunderstood or devalued you?

C. Did you have courage or lack courage to speak of God's calling?

Most of us value the approval of those we've known the longest. Jesus was first rejected by those very people. Yet his sense of calling stayed intact.

Often after we become a Christian or make a renewed commitment to Christ, people from our past may express their doubts about our changes. Our courage is deflated. Their opinions of us overwhelm the encouragement of what God is doing.

When Jesus faced similar disbelief, he persistently spoke the truth in love. He knew he wouldn't be accepted easily. People couldn't get past his image of being the town carpenter's son. Regardless of the opinions of others, he courageously stood undaunted because he knew his true identity was the Son of God. His Father's acknowledgment was sufficient.

May we courageously serve God because God's opinion of us is all we need. If God provides any affirmation from people, we can graciously accept it as God's gift. We value it but don't require it.

7. From the following passages, indicate whose affirmation Jesus does not want or need.

   A. Luke 4:40–41

   B. Luke 4:42–43

   C. Luke 5:15–16

   D. Luke 5:21–24

   E. Luke 5:27–32

8. In all these situations, how do you think Jesus persevered in staying true to his calling and not reacting in ungodly ways?

9. How do you handle the responses of others when nothing you do is considered right?

10. How do you depend upon God's acknowledgment of you more than the applause of people?

11. What empowers Jesus to stay strong in Luke 6:12?

    A. How does prayer strengthen your courage?

    B. What current challenge in your life needs prayer?

12. Read Luke 6:43–45.

    A. What is Jesus identifying within people's hearts?

    B. This is only one of many examples when Jesus challenges people about their sin and ungodly motives. What do you think he depends upon for his strength?

C. When God wanted you to confront the sin of another person, what gave you courage to obey?

13. What interesting bit of information do you find in Luke 8:1–3?

    A. How did God the Father encourage his son to stand strong?

    B. What kind of encouragement to support your courage has God given you lately?

    C. What are your thoughts about women supporting Jesus's ministry?

14. What is perplexing about the people's response to Jesus in Luke 8:33–37?

A. Why do you think Jesus wasn't discouraged even though the people rejected him?

B. If someone rejects you after you do something good, how do you feel?

C. When you've become defeated, what do you think contributes?

D. How do you fight discouragement in that situation?

15. Read Luke 9:18–22.

    A. What do you think the disciples found perplexing about Jesus's instruction?

    B. What does Jesus's command to his disciples show about his need for popularity?

C. To what degree do you feel courageous when you are popular or discouraged when you aren't?

D. Have you experienced a time when God prevented some sort of acclaim which you deserved? Explain what happened.

E. How did you stay encouraged or in what way did you lack courage to trust in God?

If a rightful recognition is withheld from us, we can't imagine why God would want us to remain silent when he could be glorified. But at times, God does withhold rightly deserved recognition even when we were going to give God the glory. The withholding might be something we do in obedience or forced upon us.

As Jesus commanded the disciples not to speak of him, there are times God knows anonymity or silence is best. God knows the time and method for maximum glory for his name. We can courageously trust him.

16. From the responses of the men in Luke 9:57–62, how do you think the human side of Jesus could have become discouraged?

The whole chapter of Luke 9 is filled with stories of people's rejection of Jesus and his good intentions for them. Any of us in those situations could easily doubt our calling or question our methods and motives. Our strength believing God's truth could wane.

But Jesus, though he had the capacity for weakness, never stumbled from choosing to do what God wanted him to do. He had complete confidence his Father's will would be perfectly fulfilled through him.

We can have a similar perseverance by not measuring our success based on the responses of others. Our success in God's eyes is based on our obedience not the results.

17. What possible temptation did Jesus resist in Luke 11:27–28?

   A. What is the connection with Luke 1:48?

   B. What truth(s) in Luke 11:27–28 did Jesus direct this woman to understand?

   C. How do you think those truths helped Jesus to not depend inordinately upon the praise of others?

D. When you fall for the temptation of depending upon the praise of people, what sinful and ungodly reactions result?

E. What Scripture(s) or biblical truth gives you courage to turn away from the temptation of people-pleasing?

The woman's comment in Luke 11:27 is both a compliment to Mary, Jesus's mother, and to Jesus himself. She is saying, "Your mother must be so happy to have a son like you. You are wonderful." She might even be insinuating Mary must be a special kind of mother to have raised such an amazing son.

Interestingly, during Jesus's ministry, Mary along with Jesus's half-siblings believed he had lost his mind (Mark 3:21). We can only wonder if in truth Mary was embarrassed to have a "son like him." Thankfully, the truths told her at Jesus's conception and birth won out, and Mary and several of Jesus's half-siblings became a part of the early church. Jesus's response to the woman indicates he didn't depend upon her recognition of his goodness, or how he was a blessing to his mother.

Jesus's dependence upon his Father's recognition can strengthen us. We don't have to be puffed up with pride hearing compliments. Jesus's focus is on those who follow God's Word. The change in other people is what thrills him and is the ultimate blessing. If we can have the same focus, we will be strong in not depending upon the comments of others—whether positive or negative.

Of course, we can receive the gratitude or acknowledgment from others. Maybe the Lord has used us to help someone—to develop their faith or encourage them. This is not wrong. Jesus knew he was the source for the change in people. God can even prompt people to encourage us.

But we will develop a spiritual kind of "idol" if we require the praise of other people for our emotional well-being. God wants to empower us to confidently let go of requiring approval by knowing God will provide everything we need, even encouragement. The ultimate blessing will be God's words when we see him in heaven, "Well done, good and faithful servant" (Matthew 25:21).

18. Read Luke 22:31–34; 54–62.

   A. In Jesus's humanity, what do you think Peter's denial meant to Jesus?

   B. Do you think Jesus knowing beforehand Peter would deny him made it harder or easier on Jesus?

   C. When someone rejects you, what message about you is presumed to be communicated? (e.g., not important, worthless, dismissible, etc.)

D. When someone rejects you, what truths give you courage to continue trusting God and know your worth and value in Christ?

19. How does Luke 22:39–46 show Jesus's humanness?

A. How does Jesus's interaction with his Father affect you?

B. What truths do you think Jesus is depending upon to stay committed?

C. What speaks to you in verse 42 adds to your strength?

D. How does Jesus deal with his disciples' inability to be supportive?

E. How does Jesus's example help you respond in a godly manner to people who disappoint you?

20. Read Luke 22:63–65 and Matthew 26:67–68. Although no one else has ever suffered emotionally from attacks on his character like Jesus has, what emotional wounds have you suffered?

Every person to some degree has experienced some kind of neglect, mistreatment, and even abuse. And unfortunately, every one of us has sinned against someone else in some way. In contrast, Jesus was completely innocent. None of us can claim that.

The Holy Spirit strengthened Jesus's steadfast allegiance to his Father, and we have the same empowering available to us, even when we are mistreated. And especially when we must ask for forgiveness for hurting others.

21. Read Luke 23:1–5.

  A. What accusations were made about Jesus?

  B. Which accusations were accurate, and which were wrong?

C. What do you think empowered Jesus to stay confident during these accusations?

D. If you are currently facing false accusations, how will Jesus's strength help you?

E. Can you share a time you were strengthened to resist defending yourself when wrongly accused?

F. What truths did you depend upon?

22. Read Luke 23:32–46.
    According to each of the following verses, how did Jesus exhibit courageous strength?

    A. v. 34

    B. v. 43

C. v. 46

23. Read Luke 24:36–44.

   A. How do you think the truth of Jesus's words in Luke 24:44 give him courageous confidence?

   B. How does Psalm 139:16 parallel this theme for our lives?

   C. How can knowing God plans to bring himself glory give you courage to obey him even if you don't know the end results?

As we have examined the courage of Jesus, we can be inspired knowing the same courage God made available to his Son is the same courage he offers us. We have the Holy Spirit within us to give us everything we need.

Even though we have everything we need available to us, we can be comforted knowing God doesn't expect us to be perfect. Knowing God has realistic expectations of us prevents discouragement. He will continue to help us walk in his power.

My Precious Princess and Daughter,

You are a woman of courage. I see you through the lens of the royal righteous robe given to you through my Son.

As your God who knows everything, I am not dismayed or discouraged by your struggle. From eternity when I designed the plan of salvation, I knew only my Son would be the perfect human. I created this plan so you could give up your plan to be perfect in order to earn my love.

Be encouraged. I've done what you can't. I've completed the way for humans to gain access to me through Jesus dying on the cross in your place. If I've arranged the ultimate sacrifice, then I can do all things to help you grow. Your perfection is not my goal. Growth is. Growth means you will continue to need me, and you will draw closer to me. Intimacy with you is what I love.

Depend upon me. I'm your only hope of steadfast support. I love you.

Lovingly,
Your Heavenly Father, the King

About the Author

Kathy Collard Miller is best known for her practical biblical teaching with vulnerable sharing, humor, and motivation woven throughout her speaking and writing. Her ministry began when God delivered her from the sin of abuse of her toddler daughter and restored her broken marriage to Larry.

Her first book telling her story was published in 1984 and now has been revised and expanded as *No More Anger: Hope for an Out-of-Control Mom*.

Since her first book was published, Kathy has been in awe of God's plan to develop a ministry with a worldwide impact. She is the bestselling and award-winning author of over fifty-five books, which feature a full array of nonfiction genres including Bible studies, Bible commentaries, and Christian living topics, and has also been an editor of compilation books.

Along with her Daughters of the King Bible Study Series, one of her popular books is *Pure-Hearted: The Blessings of Living Out God's Glory*.

Kathy and her husband, Larry, have written many books together including *God's Intriguing Questions: 40 Old Testament Devotions Revealing God's Nature*, *God's Intriguing Questions: 60 New Testament Devotions Revealing Jesus's Nature*, and *Never Ever Be the Same: A New You Starts Today*.

Kathy's articles have appeared in numerous magazines and online sources. She has appeared on hundreds of radio and television programs including The 700 Club.

Kathy is also amazed about the open doors God has given her for speaking. She has spoken in more than thirty US states and nine foreign countries including China, Indonesia, and Greece. She loves to see new sights and is so grateful her ministry allows her to travel and see the world.

Kathy and Larry, her husband, high school sweethearts who married in 1970, both lay counselors, often write and speak together, especially at marriage events. Kathy and Larry live in Boise, Idaho, and are the parents of two and grandparents of two.

www.KathyCollardMiller.com
Facebook:www.facebook.com/KathyCollardMillerAuthor
Twitter: @KathyCMiller
Pinterest/Kathyspeak
Youtube: https://bit.ly/2SwiL03
Instagram: @kathycollardmiller
Amazon author page: https://www.amazon.com/Kathy-Collard-Miller/e/B001KMI1oS?

Endnotes

Lesson 3

1. (Quoted in *The Divine Conspiracy* by Dallas Willard, HarperSanFrancisco, 1997, NY NY. pg. 65-66. Referenced to John M'Clintock and James Strong, eds. *Cyclopaedia of Biblical, Theological, and Ecclesiastical Literature*, vol. 3 (New York: Harper & Brothers, 1894), pg. 903-4.)

Books by Kathy Collard Miller with Elk Lake Publishing, Inc.

Christian Living Books:
Pure-Hearted: The Blessings of Living Out God's Glory
No More Anger: Hope for an Out-of-Control Mom
God's Intriguing Questions: 40 Old Testament Devotions Revealing God's Nature
God's Intriguing Questions: 60 New Testament Devotions Revealing Jesus's Nature
Daughters of the King Bible study series:

- *Choices of the Heart*: ten lessons about the women of the Bible, contrasting two different women of the Bible about one topic in each lesson.
- *Whispers of My Heart*: ten lessons about prayer.
- *At the Heart of Friendship*: ten lessons about different aspects of relationships.
- *Heart Wisdom*: ten lessons about different topics covered in the biblical book of Proverbs.
- *Heart of Courage*: ten lessons guiding and inspiring the student to exhibit courageous trust and action in God's power and wisdom.
- More books on other topics in the series will be coming.

www.ingramcontent.com/pod-product-compliance
Lightning Source LLC
Chambersburg PA
CBHW060516090426
42735CB00011B/2255